PARALLEL PARKING IS EASY

(AND OTHER LIES)

PARALLEL PARKING
IS EASY
(AND OTHER LIES)

EVERYTHING NEW DRIVERS NEED TO KNOW
TO STAY SAFE AND SMART ON THE ROAD

KRISTY GRANT

ULYSSES PRESS

Published in the US by
ULYSSES PRESS
PO Box 3440
Berkeley, CA 94703
www.ulyssespress.com

ISBN: 978-1-64604-159-6
Library of Congress Control Number: 2020947023

Printed in the United States by Kingery Printing Company
10 9 8 7 6 5 4 3 2 1

Artwork all from shutterstock.com: © Balabolka except pages 5, 37, 79, 123 © Kovalov Anatolii (arrow); page 7 © Dustik (cleaner); page 8 © Rvector (card); page 101 © Prokhorovich (fox); pages 108 and 134 © Elena Pimukova (light, arrows); page 137 © wenchiawang (light with people) and © Visual Generation (motorcycle); page 139 © hchjjl (dump truck); page 141 © Netkoff (ambulance); page 142 © K.Sorokin (fire truck); page 142 © Visual Generation (tractor); page 146 © Janis Abolins (flat tire); page 152 © Aleks Melnik (hat); page 153 © bsd (car); page 154 © stas (penalty); page 155 © Pavel Mastepanov (balance); page 157 © K.Sorokin (crash cars); page 169 © Alex Blogoodf (pillow wheel)

NOTE TO READERS: Neither the author nor the publisher is engaged in rendering professional advice to the individual reader. Learning to drive requires supervision by a qualified adult. This handbook is not a substitute for consulting with a professional driving instructor, learning the laws of your state, or using your own common sense and judgment while in a vehicle. Neither the author nor the publisher shall be liable or responsible for any loss or damage allegedly arising from any information or suggestion in this book.

CONTENTS

SECTION 3

SECTION 4

THIS BOOK BELONGS TO:

_____

INTRODUCTION

You Got Your License... Congrats! (Now What?)

Everyone has an opinion when they find out you're a new driver. That includes driving instructors, family members, and even friends who have only been driving for a hot second longer than you. It's a lot to process, and the sheer amount of information can make anyone a little nervous about their first solo trips. But it doesn't have to be that way. To help you navigate those first months on the road, we've gathered the most useful, practical, and surprising tips we could find, then squeezed them all into this book. Read it, highlight it, then stow it in the glove box of whatever vehicle you'll be driving. Just knowing it's right there can help you feel better prepared whenever you get behind the wheel.

HOW TO NAVIGATE THIS BOOK...

Each chapter has a few small items that are meant to help you tackle some of the toughest or most important topics. For example:

Q&A: ASK YOURSELF: Answer these questions honestly to make sure you're on the right track—and see what to do next.

Q&A: ASK SOMEONE ELSE: Ask a parent, guardian, or driving instructor these questions to show you value their opinion—and get info you can't find on your own.

MYTHS & TRUTHS: Here, we debunk common myths about driving—and tell you what you really need to know instead.

FACTS & STATS: Knowing certain numbers is vital for safe (and legal) driving. Here, we call out ones that really count.

CHECK IT OUT: You can put the book's tips to use easily by following these straightforward checklists.

SECTION 1

ALL REVVED UP: PREP YOUR CAR (AND YOURSELF)

Unless your family is in the auto business, they may not know as much about cars as you might think. Your household also may not realize they need to explain what they expect from you in terms of money, safety, and responsibilities. These chapters will help you get yourself up to speed—and ready to hit the road.

➤ CHAPTER 1:

Get in Gear: Essentials (and Extras) to Keep in Your Car

It's time to hit the road. Stocking your vehicle with important tools, gear, and extras can help you feel more confident and prepared. It also shows that you're taking this seriously, which might ease your parents' minds, too. Even if you'll be driving a family car, you might be surprised at what items *aren't* in the trunk or glove box. After all, phone chargers probably weren't a "thing" when your parents got their licenses. That said, here's what experts suggest today's drivers keep in their cars.

START IN THE AUTOMOTIVE DEPARTMENT

Even if you have a roadside assistance plan, you might get stuck having to change your own tire or jumpstart your car, so make sure your trunk is stocked with a jack, a lug wrench, and an inflated (not flat) spare tire. Consider getting some jumper cables or, better yet, a portable car battery charger. The former will require you to hook up to another car, but the charger is something you can use all on your own. The manufacturers of these items often post videos online that show how to use them.

Stats & Facts

STAT: One third of cars made in 2018 have "nearly unbreakable" windows.

FACT: A vehicle escape tool, which has a window-breaker and a seat-belt cutter, can help you make a fast exit, if needed.

VISIT THE PHARMACY, TOO

It's a good idea to keep basics like tissues and hand sanitizer in the car for when you have a cold or want to clean up before getting dinner at the drive-through. Also stow a ready-made first-aid kit in the trunk, or make your own kit using instructions from the American Red Cross (redcross.org). If you have any medical conditions (like diabetes or asthma), consider getting medical ID jewelry—or tuck a note in your wallet that lists them and any important medications. This can be helpful to medical professionals, whether you faint in gym class or get into a fender bender.

TAKE A DETOUR TO THE ELECTRONICS AISLE

Of course, a cell phone cable and adapter are a must wherever you go. Note that the electric-plug type won't work in cars, so you'll need a cigarette-lighter adapter instead. For long trips, take a portable power charger along, too. Just remember that technology is not always reliable. When you're going on a long trip, download a map and directions so you can pull over and check them if you're in a dead zone. Also keep a list of important phone numbers in your wallet (for people you'd call if you need help), in case you need to use someone else's device.

OPEN YOUR WALLET AND GLOVE BOX

You should always have your driver's license and auto insurance card in your wallet—and in your possession while driving. Most people keep the car registration in the glove box. To make it easier to find if you get pulled over, store it in a brightly colored envelope. If the owner's manual contains a spare key or any identifying information (like the car's VIN number), store those at home, but leave the book in the glove box. Download a *digital* manual from the car manufacture's website, too, since it will be easier to search for things like "how to change the dashboard clock." Need prescription lenses to drive? Stash an extra pair of contact lenses or prescription glasses in your glove box (or backpack) so you can get home even if you break or lose the ones you're wearing.

KNOW WHEN TO CLEAN IT OUT

When you start taking on passengers, you'll want to have a place for them to sit. But that's not the only reason to de-clutter the car every so often. Envelopes, papers, cash, bags, packages, and other items can attract unwanted attention. (Even without anything visible, some people consider an unlocked car to be fair game, so always lock the doors when you're not sitting inside the car.)

Another rule worth making for yourself and, eventually, anyone you transport: Don't leave leftover food and food wrappers in the car, even overnight. These can attract pests like ants or mice. Getting rid of *those* is harder (and more disgusting) than tossing out the trash.

Q&A: Ask Yourself

☐ What other items might I want to keep in my car (like sports gear)?

☐ Do I know how to find and use all of the items in my car? If not, who can help me?

☐ Which items should I store in a bin or bag to make them easier to find or move?

☐ How will I remind myself to test things like flashlight batteries and tire pressure?

Q&A: Ask Someone Else

☐ Who should I call if I need roadside assistance? What is the phone number?

☐ What **other** items do my parents or family members keep in their cars?

☐ What time of year should I change out seasonal items?

CHECK IT OUT: WHAT TO STASH IN YOUR CAR

Here's a quick reference that summarizes the tips from this chapter, plus a few other helpful items worth having in your vehicle. (You can share this with relatives who want to get you a helpful, practical gift.)

IN YOUR WALLET

- ○ Auto insurance card
- ○ Cash and/or a credit/debit/gas card
- ○ Driver's license
- ○ Health insurance cards
- ○ List of health conditions/medications
- ○ List of important phone numbers
- ○ Roadside assistance card

ON THE WINDSHIELD/WINDOWS

- ○ Electronic toll collection reader
- ○ Roadside assistance provider's sticker
- ○ Parking sticker and/or pass
- ○ Inspection sticker (in applicable states)

IN THE CONSOLE OR DOOR POCKET

- ○ Hand sanitizer
- ○ Phone charging cable and car charger adaptor
- ○ Portable power charger (for phone)
- ○ Sunglasses that block UVA/UVB rays
- ○ Tissues
- ○ Vehicle escape tool

IN THE GLOVE BOX

- O Air pressure gauge
- O Backup pair of prescription glasses and/or contact lenses
- O Car registration (in a bright envelope)
- O Flashlight and extra batteries
- O Multipurpose tool or Swiss army knife
- O Owner's manual
- O Pen/pencil and notepaper

IN THE TRUNK

- O Blanket and/or large towel
- O Car jack
- O Something to brace one of the wheels while changing a flat (wedges, bricks, wheel chocks)
- O First-aid kit
- O Jumper cables
- O Lug wrench
- O Portable car battery charger
- O Reusable shopping bags
- O Spare tire, inflated

IN A "SEASONAL GEAR" BOX

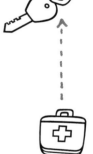

- O For winter: Ice scraper/brush, small shovel, ice melt, winter hat, gloves, boots, blanket
- O For summer: Sunscreen, bug spray, towels
- O Umbrella

AT HOME

- O Car title
- O Owner's manual (digital version)
- O Records of service, repairs, and warranties
- O Spare key and/or remote

➤ CHAPTER 2:
A Quick Guide to Dashboard Lights

Many new drivers don't notice the symbols on the dashboard when they light up. Other people ignore them because they think someone else (like their parents) will take care of it. But this can be bad for the car or the passengers, depending on what's lit.

Whenever you drive *any* car, look at the dashboard after starting it up. If you see a colorful symbol and you don't know what it means, double-check the owner's manual to find out what to do. You can also ask someone who knows the car well or search online (or in the glove box) for a quick-start guide, which will share this info plus helpful tips on where to find things like the release for the gas-cap cover.

Here are a few of the most important types of dashboard lights, what they typically look like, and what they mean.

SEAT BELT NOT FASTENED

WHAT IT LOOKS LIKE: A seated person wearing a seat belt

WHAT TO DO ABOUT IT: If you turn on the car and don't fasten your seat belt, this light will flash. If you start to drive over 15 miles per hour, you'll hear a warning sound, too. To prevent all of that, just buckle up as soon as you've adjusted your seat and before you shift out of Park.

PRO TIP: Keep in mind that the seat belt is designed to be worn across the chest and pelvis (*not* tucked under your arm). If it cuts into your neck, get a seat belt strap pad to cushion it. If it's too tight, get a seat belt extender. (Sometimes a car can be outfitted with a seat belt adjuster by the manufacturer.)

Stats & Facts

STAT: 91% of Americans wear their seat belts.

FACT: You're not a dork if you wear your seat belt. In fact, most of the people you know wear theirs, too. That's good, because, in 2017, nearly half of the people who died in crashes weren't wearing a seat belt.

PASSENGER-SIDE AIRBAG OFF

WHAT IT LOOKS LIKE: A seated person in side view wearing a seat belt with a circle (airbag) in front of their face

WHAT TO DO ABOUT IT: Cars with airbags automatically sense how much weight is in the front passenger seat. If the person is small enough to be injured by an airbag, the car will set the airbag to open with less force (or not at all) if there's a crash. People who are this small (and anyone under age 13) will be safer if they ride in the back.

PRO TIP: If something like a backpack is "riding" on the passenger seat, it can cause the light to come on (which of course is OK).

Myths & Truths

MYTH: Airbags are enough to protect you.

TRUTH: Airbags are designed to work along *with* seat belts. In fact, you can get injured badly if an airbag opens and you're *not* buckled up. Wearing your seat belt is the best way to protect yourself in a crash.

OPEN DOOR OR TRUNK

WHAT IT LOOKS LIKE: An overhead view of a vehicle with open doors

WHAT TO DO ABOUT IT: It's easy to forget to shut a door or the trunk. Or sometimes you'll think it's closed but it's not *latched*. If that happens, this light will let you know about it.

PRO TIP: Put the car in Park and turn it off before getting out to see which door needs to be slammed again. When you do, check to make sure nothing (like a seat belt or junk) is blocking the way.

LOW WINDSHIELD-WASHER FLUID

WHAT IT LOOKS LIKE: A windshield with spouting fluid

WHAT TO DO ABOUT IT: Being low on washer fluid may not seem like a big deal, but it can actually be dangerous. For example, what if your windshield gets unexpectedly spattered with mud while you're driving? Leaving it empty for too long can also cause the system to wear out more quickly. Bottom line: Fill it up ASAP. It's inexpensive and easy to do yourself, using the car manual as a guide.

PRO TIP: If this light is on, don't try to use the washer fluid. Running it on empty can wear out the pump. Also, if you live in a cold climate, be sure to choose washer fluid that contains antifreeze.

LOW FUEL

WHAT IT LOOKS LIKE: A gas pump

WHAT TO DO ABOUT IT: On some cars, this light tells you
when the gas tank is getting low, while on other cars it tells you how
many gallons (and/or miles of driving) you have left. Either way, it's
better to refuel *before* you go below a quarter of a tank of gas. This amount of
fuel helps protect the fuel pump from overheating in summer and from forming
ice crystals in winter.

PRO TIP: There is usually a gas pump picture (not light) on your gas gauge,
too. If there's an arrow next to this symbol, it's telling you which side of the
vehicle the gas cap is on.

LOW TIRE PRESSURE

WHAT IT LOOKS LIKE: The bottom part of a flat tire with an
exclamation point in the center

WHAT TO DO ABOUT IT: Don't ignore this! It might mean you have a nail
in your tire, or it could be that you need to add air because of a change in the
weather. You can add air for free at most gas stations, using the directions on
the pump. You'll find the correct "psi" (pounds per square inch) on a sticker on
the driver's door frame or in the manual. But if this light keeps coming on, have a
mechanic check to make sure there's not a nail in your tire.

PRO TIP: Don't drive on a flat tire for any longer than you have to. It can
reduce gas mileage, cause tires to wear unevenly, or even cause a tire to fail,
possibly causing an accident.

CHECK ENGINE

WHAT IT LOOKS LIKE: A car engine (or words like "service engine soon")

WHAT TO DO ABOUT IT: This symbol means there's something wrong
with the car. It could be just a minor issue or something more serious. You won't
know which it is until you take the vehicle to a mechanic, who can use a decoder
to diagnose the problem. If this light is flashing, though, don't drive the car at all!

It usually means there's been an engine misfire, and if you keep going, you could wreck the catalytic converter. That can be expensive or impossible to fix.

PRO TIP: Check the gas cap to make sure it's tightened properly. (Unscrew it and put it back on again.) If that was the problem, the light will go off after 10 or 20 miles of driving.

HIGH BEAMS

WHAT IT LOOKS LIKE: A squid or rocket moving sideways

WHAT TO DO ABOUT IT: Use your high beams only if you're alone on the road and click them off as soon as you see another vehicle approaching.

PRO TIP: If other drivers are flashing their lights at you, it may be because you have your high beams on or you have forgotten to turn on your own lights. (Other times, it means there is a speed trap or other problem ahead.)

STABILITY CONTROL

WHAT IT LOOKS LIKE: A rear view of a car with squiggly tire tracks behind it

WHAT TO DO ABOUT IT: If this comes on, it means that your car's traction control system is trying to keep your tires from slipping. This can happen when you're driving on an icy or wet road. If this comes on, don't panic—use the tips in Chapter 18 for driving in bad weather.

PRO TIP: This light will turn off on its own once your vehicle is back under control. If it does not, ask a certified technician to check if there's a faulty sensor or other problem.

FINAL THOUGHT: WHEN THE DASHBOARD LIGHTS "LIE"

Sometimes, a light goes on (or stays on), even when nothing is wrong with the car. For example, even if all of the doors are shut, the open-door indicator might "think" that they're not. When this happens, it might be due to a problem with the car's computer or the switch. Again, don't guess (or assume it's OK). Ask a certified technician to figure it out.

Q&A: Ask Yourself

- ☐ Have I looked at the owner's manual to see what the dashboard symbols look like on my car?

- ☐ Do I know what each of them means?

- ☐ Do I make it a habit to check them each time I start the car?

Q&A: Ask Someone Else

- ☐ Who should I tell if a light comes on when I start the car?

- ☐ Who should I call if I am already on the road?

- ☐ Do I have a roadside assistance plan for myself or my car?

Save the sleek ride for your twenties: You're four times less likely to get in a fender bender at that age. To keep yourself safer now (and to keep your insurance premium as low as possible), look at these features when car shopping:

1. Speed & style. New drivers are more likely to speed in a "sports car." This is one reason they cost more to insure. For your first ride, look for a car with 200 horsepower (or as low as possible). If you'd call it a "sports car," it's not a good fit.

2. Size & weight. Your best bet? Mid- and full-size passenger cars. Young drivers are less likely to crash bigger, heavier vehicles—and if they do, they're better protected than they would be in a compact car. Avoid pickup trucks or SUVs, though, which are too easy to roll over.

3. Safety & comfort. Older cars often cost less to insure but they also lack some safety features. Ideally, you'll want a car with automatic stability/traction control, anti-lock brakes, and airbags. (It's even better if there are also airbags for passengers.) Some cars are kinder to the climate than others, too. For the official U.S. government safety ratings *and* environmental ratings of new and used cars from 1984 to now, download the Find-a-Car mobile app from the EPA website fueleconomy.gov.

Also make sure the car fits you physically. Can you adjust the seat and steering wheel so you are comfortable, can see well, and can reach the pedals and controls properly? Having everything in the right place can help you with reaction time when driving.

4. Accidents & recalls. If buying a used car, look it up on CARFAX.com or AutoCheck.com. These sites offer reports that tell you if it has been in an accident or if there are recalls on it, if the airbags have been deployed, and lots of other info. If there are red flags, take it to a trusted mechanic before you buy it!

5. Interior & exterior color. Though lots of people swear that certain paint colors are safer, there's not much research to back that up. The car's color usually won't wreck your insurance rate either, even if you choose red.

Do keep in mind that dark-colored vinyl or leather interiors get hotter in summer than light-colored fabric seats. Bottom line, though: Pick what you like (or whatever is the best deal).

AT A GLANCE: WHAT TO LOOK FOR IN A CAR

- O Mid-size or full-size sedan
- O 200 horsepower (or as low as possible)
- O Anti-lock brakes
- O Airbags (as many as possible)
- O Automatic stability/traction control
- O High safety ratings from the National Highway Traffic Safety Administration (NHTSA) and the Insurance Institute for Highway Safety (IIHS)
- O Adjustable seats, adjustable steering wheel, etc.
- O Good fuel economy and EPA emissions ratings
- O Whatever colors and materials you like best

➤ CHAPTER 3:

Test Your Tech: GPS, Music, and More

Here's another lie adults tell you (and themselves): Teens are the most-distracted drivers. The low-key truth is that many adults are *terrible* about multitasking—especially with car tech.

This is one area where you can flex: After you figure out the tech for your car, phone, and other devices, you can teach the adults in your life how everything works. (It feels good to be the expert on something.)

Since every car is different, this chapter just talks about what *types* of tech you might want to try first. You can search online to find manuals and videos that offer specifics on the brands you buy.

PLUG IN WITH THE RIGHT ACCESSORIES

It's best not to deal with your phone while driving—even using hands-free mode. But you may need to charge your phone in the car. Some vehicles made after 2013 have built-in USB ports. If your car doesn't, you'll need a USB adapter for the car's cigarette lighter. This lets you charge up using the same cable you use to connect your phone to your computer.

PRO TIP: Unplug the phone charger when you're not using it, especially if your car battery is low. Even when there's no phone attached, it drains the battery when the car is not running. (When the car *is* running, the charger uses energy from gas.)

Stats & Facts

STAT: Reaction time is delayed by 25% when people use voice-to-text devices.

FACT: Other voice-activated apps and GPS systems are equally distracting. Just because you *can* do something doesn't mean it's a good idea.

SET THE CLOCK TO THE CORRECT TIME

Some people *never* change their car's clock. This can make you think you're running an hour late (or early) when you're not. That's stress you don't need right now.

Even if your car's clock resets itself (using a satellite), you still might need to choose the right time zone, using the digital display. Older cars may have a set of buttons labeled H and M for hour and minute.

PRO TIP: If you fix the clock in someone else's car, let them know: They may be used to "doing the math" (adding or subtracting an hour). You don't want them to be late (or early) because you were trying to be helpful.

MAKE SURE YOU CAN HEAR YOURSELF THINK

Anything that comes out of the car's speakers—music, phone calls, GPS directions—can startle you if it's too loud. And one study showed that music over 95 decibels can slow a driver's reaction time by up to 20%. Turning down the volume also makes it easier to hear horns and sirens. If you're not sure what "too loud" means, download a decibel-measuring app to use as a guide.

If your car has a digital display, it probably has a menu in the "settings" where you can adjust the volume. Sometimes you can set the volume at different levels for phone calls, map directions, and music. If not, look for a volume knob.

PRO TIP: If you do turn up the volume when you're sitting in a parked car, turn it back down before shutting off the car. The next driver won't appreciate getting bombarded unexpectedly when they turn the key. (And you won't get bombarded with a lecture about it.)

TRY TO PAIR THE BLUETOOTH SYSTEM

Don't assume that every car's Bluetooth system will work with your phone. To find out if your phone and your car's Bluetooth system *should* be compatible, check the car manufacturer's website for a section on "Bluetooth compatibility." They'll usually provide a list of phones that will pair with that car. Keep in mind, though, that software upgrades can cause a new glitch. So it's best to try to pair your phone with a car's Bluetooth system before you purchase or drive it.

Don't stress if your car *doesn't* have a Bluetooth system. Most cars can have a unit installed as an add-on. Again, make sure your phone works with that particular system *before* the installer rips up the dashboard.

PRO TIP: If you pair your phone with someone else's car (including a rental), be sure to clear your phone from the computer's history afterward. Also do this if you pair your phone with a car you're test-driving or selling.

Myths & Truths

MYTH: It's always legal to use hands-free devices.

TRUTH: For drivers under 18, some states don't allow the use of *any* wireless devices while driving. This means no voice-activated texting or hands-free cell phone calls at all. Even if your state hasn't made it illegal to use wireless devices while driving, it's a good idea to act as if it did. Talking on the phone is distracting, especially if the subject matter is, too.

ANOTHER SURPRISE: Using voice-to-text is actually *more* distracting than typing a text message. (Of course, you should never do that either.)

EXPLORE THE OPTIONS FOR DIGITAL NAVIGATION

It's best to stick to familiar roads for your first solo trips (to lower the stress level). But it's smart to know how GPS works in case you wind up lost. So ask an adult if you can try it out while they're driving.

Many people simply use a maps app on their phone. There are basic apps like Google Maps but there are also apps like Waze that will alert you to accidents, speed traps, and other issues.

Some cars have a built-in navigation system (and a separate manual on it). But you may still prefer to use an app. Some built-in systems need to be upgraded every few years and if yours isn't, it may not "know" all the changes that have happened to the roads.

PRO TIP: If you're selling a car (or returning a rental car), delete any addresses you added to its built-in navigation system, especially if there's one called "Home."

CALM DOWN (OR PAUSE) YOUR PLAYLIST

As a new driver, it's best to wait a few months before you add background music to your driving. But it's good to know how things work so you can take over as DJ when you're riding with a more experienced driver. So once your phone is paired, you can test out Spotify while parked in the driveway.

If you do want music on while you drive, don't play your favorites. In a study of teen drivers, 98% made driving mistakes while listening to their own music. Seventeen of them actually needed a driving instructor to take over the controls to prevent a crash. Soft rock, light jazz, or easy listening did not have that effect, though you may prefer silence to any of those.

PRO TIP: Research online to see if your favorite music app offers features or modes that make for safer driving. For example, Spotify launched Car View mode in 2019. It jacks up the size of the most important buttons so they're easier to see. Spotify is also looking into adding voice controls.

TAKE YOUR BACKUP CAMERA FOR A TEST DRIVE

Many cars have a backup camera that comes on when you shift the car into Reverse. Its screen may be on the console, dashboard, rearview mirror, or sun visor. These cameras give you a wide view of what's behind your car. Some also show you (using red, yellow, and green lines and arrows, for example) how far you are from what's behind you. So if you're in the green, you should be fine, but as you enter yellow, you're getting close to whatever is behind you. There may be sensors in the rear bumper that check for items behind the car or traffic coming from either direction (like when you're backing out of a parking space).

Even if you have this and learn how to use it, don't rely only on your backup camera. It can miss low-to-the-ground objects, among other things. Before you shift into Reverse, check all the way around your car to make sure no objects or people are in your way. Shift into Reverse to activate the camera, while keeping your foot on the brake. And keep looking over each shoulder and using all your mirrors. Basically, the camera is just giving you another set of eyes—it's not replacing what you usually would do.

PUT YOUR PHONE TO SLEEP AUTOMATICALLY

Most phones have a setting that will block phone calls and texts while you are driving. (For instance, the iPhone has a mode called Do Not Disturb While Driving.) These can usually be set to turn on automatically when your phone senses the car is in motion. That's great because it's one less thing to think about when you get in the car.

Many phones and safe-driving apps will even auto-reply to people who try to contact you while you're driving. But they also let important calls through when the caller is on your "favorites" list or calls three times in a row, for example. Parents and insurance companies love these options, and you probably will, too. It's nice to get away from friend drama, even if it's just for a hot second.

CHECK IT OUT: YOUR QUICK TECH DOUBLECHECK

Here's the short version of this chapter. Use it to make
sure you have the digital setup you need to succeed.

BEFORE YOU GO FOR A DRIVE:

○ Test your phone charger to make sure it still works.

○ Set the car's clock if you have time.

○ Turn down the volume, if needed.

○ Put your destination address into your GPS if you need to use it.

○ Set your phone to sleep if it doesn't do it on its own.

BEFORE YOU RETURN OR SELL A CAR:

○ Unplug your phone charger and cable.

○ Unpair your phone if you won't be in that car again.

○ Turn down the volume if you turned it up.

○ Delete personal info from the car's computer, including GPS
and Bluetooth.

➤ CHAPTER 4:

Start Off in the Right Direction: How to Deal with Your Parents

Some people say, "It's easier to ask for forgiveness than for permission." But that's not the best strategy when you're taking control of something weighing more than 4,000 pounds. When it comes to driving, it's easier to come to an agreement on the terms up front (and put them in writing).

Understanding everyone's expectations can prevent future arguments about things like whose turn it is to borrow the car or fill the gas tank. It can also help you budget for whatever costs will fall on you. Turning this into a contract means you have some official rules to follow, which takes some of the weight off your shoulders. (For example, if you've agreed not to have passengers, you won't have to decide whether to give someone a ride.)

To make it easier, you can just download a driving contract from the Internet. But still make sure you cover the following topics when you go over it with your family.

LOOK UP THE NEW-LICENSE LAWS

Most states have Graduated Driver Licensing (GDL) laws, which ease teens into driving. Typically, you start with a learner's permit, then get an intermediate or junior license after passing a road test, then graduate to a regular or unrestricted license at age 18 (if your driving record is good). At each phase, there are different things you are allowed to do (or not). For example, many states restrict how many young passengers a new driver can transport, as well as what times of day you are legally allowed to be on the road. These restrictions are meant to prevent some of the most common causes of teen accidents, so don't brush them off. Visit your state's Department of Transportation website to find its specific GDL laws and include them in your contract.

CONSIDER AN EARLY-ISH CURFEW

It's safer for you to have a curfew because most of the deadly crashes by teen drivers happen between 9 p.m. and midnight. Many GDL laws will require you to be off the road by 11 p.m. anyway. (Tip: Set a reminder on your phone an hour before your curfew.)

If you're sharing a car, also discuss when you will be able to use it. (After school? On weekends? For work?) And find out how much advance notice you need to give. (An hour? A day? A week?) Have a lot of drivers for one vehicle? Use a digital calendar or sign-up app to keep track.

GET PASSENGERS PREAPPROVED

Again, GDL laws may regulate how many people you can take—and common sense says it's best to drive solo for a while so you can focus. But even if you're allowed one passenger, your parents may want to know who it will be. (We all have some friends who are . . . distracting.)

This is also a good time to ask your parents if they are expecting you to chauffeur anyone. For example, will you be their designated driver or will you need to take your siblings to sports practice? If you aren't comfortable with their expectations, now is the time to talk about it.

REVIEW YOUR UPCOMING ROUTES

Some intersections are especially busy or difficult to navigate. Some roads are windy or in bad shape. Some highways might be worth avoiding at first. Take advantage of your parents' driving experience and ask which routes they suggest you take (or avoid).

An even simpler approach would be to agree to just a few routes for starters, such as to school, a friend's house, and work. Then map out those routes with your parents and don't drive anywhere else until you feel more confident behind the wheel.

DO THE MATH ON EXPECTED EXPENSES

As a new driver, you may have no idea what car-related things cost. Refueling can cost $20 or more. An oil change can cost up to $50 (or more). And car insurance costs thousands. And then there are fees like parking permits, highway or bridge tolls, and car registration.

Before you think of getting your *own* car, look at how much money you have and/or earn—and how much of that can realistically go to these expenses. You might find you can cover the car payment but not the rest of it. If it's a shared vehicle, find out how much of the expenses will be your responsibility. You may need to give up some splurges like concert tix or gourmet coffee for a while.

SPELL OUT YOUR ROAD-SAFETY PLAN

Obviously, you are planning to be safe on the road. Still, your loved ones will worry less if you officially *promise* to do certain things. This includes following all laws (speed limits, seat-belt laws, GDL laws, etc.) and promising not to drive distracted, tired, angry, or otherwise impaired. Also agree to tell them where you're going, to call when you get there, and to let them know when you're heading home.

Having this on paper also gives you something to show your *friends* when they want you to do something risky. You can tell them, "If I don't follow this contract, I can't drive the car anymore."

Stats & Facts

STAT: 41% of teens say their parents practice unsafe driving habits, even after their teens ask them to stop.

FACT: If your parents just won't listen to you, remind them of this: Surveys show that teens whose parents set good examples when driving are less likely to take risks or get in a crash.

DEFINE WHAT "CLEAN" MEANS

"Clean" means different things to different people. Some people allow no food or drink in the car at all. (You shouldn't be having any food or drink while driving, but it may be off-limits to passengers, too.) People who drive on dirt roads may be used to a dusty exterior. At a minimum, make sure the windshield washer fluid isn't empty. In fact, make sure all the windows and mirrors are clean. Beyond that, find out how often the car should be cleaned (inside and out), who is supposed to do that, and (if it's you) if you can do it yourself or should take it to a car wash.

ASK FOR A SOMETHING IN RETURN

Most contracts include some give and take. So think about what you need from the adults and other drivers in your house. Do you still need help practicing parallel parking, highway driving, or driving at night or in bad weather? Ask for an experienced driver to commit to working with you a little each week.

Also ask for support if you wind up in a tough situation. For example, if you're too tired or otherwise unfit to drive, let them know you want to be able to call for help—without getting yelled at right away. Promise you'll face the consequences, but you don't want to be afraid to reach out.

AGREE TO FACE THE CONSEQUENCES

Your parents will respect your request for a contract, but you have to take it seriously after it's signed. Of course you don't want to slip up, but you should also find out what happens if you do. For example, discuss the additional penalty if you get a ticket, have a fender bender, break curfew, forget to fill up the tank, etc. If any of those things happen, don't try to talk your way out of it—instead, apologize and explain what you'll do differently in the future.

All of this will go a long way toward building your parents' confidence in you. That way, when you sit down in a few months to review the driving contract, you can ask them to let you do more—like drive more often and take more passengers.

CHECK IT OUT: SUGGESTIONS FOR YOUR CONTRACT

Below are some of the things you might want to include
in your driving contract. This is just an example. Be
sure to adjust it to suit your personal needs.

GENERAL

O I will follow all the laws of my state, including Graduated Driver
Licensing laws.

O I will obey all traffic signs and signals.

O If I have a question about a rule or law, I will look it up in my
state's driver's manual.

O I will not let anyone else drive the car without specific
permission from my parents.

O I will fill up the tank when _____.

TIMING

O I will ask for permission to use the vehicle this much in
advance: _____.

O I will drive only between these hours: _____.

O My curfew is: _____.

O I will make every effort to be home before my curfew. If
something prevents this, I will call ASAP. I will not speed or
drive unsafely to make it back before curfew.

DESTINATION

O I will drive only to agreed-upon destinations. These include:

_____

_____.

O I will always let an adult know where I am going, what route I will
be taking, when I arrive, when I plan to return, and when I leave
to head home. I will do this whether I am a driver or a passenger.

○ I will figure out how much time it will take to reach a destination, then leave at *least* 15 minutes earlier than that, so I do not feel rushed.

○ If I *am* running late, I will *not* rush to arrive on time. I will accept that I will arrive late, if necessary, so I can drive safely and calmly.

PASSENGERS

○ I will only drive with the agreed-upon number of passengers in the car. This is: _____.

○ I will only drive with passengers my parents have approved. This includes:

_____

_____.

○ I will make sure that the passenger gets their parents' permission before riding with me.

○ I will make sure my passengers wear their seat belt and are otherwise acting safely.

○ I will not engage in reckless driving, even if a passenger pressures me to do so. If a passenger is a problem or distraction, I will not let them ride with me again.

○ I will never ride *as a passenger* with a driver who is unsafe to drive.

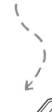

DISTRACTIONS

○ I will not eat, drink, smoke, or vape when driving.

○ I will not allow illegal items or substances in the car at any time.

○ I will not use my phone (including Bluetooth and hands-free) while driving.

○ I will only program my GPS or music when parked and in a safe location. I will not use GPS or music for the first _____ months of driving alone.

○ I will not do *anything* distracting while on the road, like putting on makeup or looking for something in my backpack. I will not even do this when stopped at a light or stop sign.

○ I will tell my passengers they must not do anything to distract me.

COSTS

○ I will pay for these things: _____

_____.

PROBLEMS

○ I will not drive the car if a dashboard light indicates it is unsafe. (See Chapter 2.)

○ I will not drive in unsafe weather conditions.

○ I will not drive if I am impaired *in any way*, including being upset, tired, or angry.

○ I will not try to hide a warning, ticket, or accident from my parents.

○ I will call for help right away if I have a problem with the car or with driving.

○ I will welcome my parent to ride as a passenger at any time for any reason in order to check my driving skills.

CONSEQUENCES

○ Breaking any of the rules marked with an asterisk (*) will result in lost driving privileges for ___ days/weeks/months.

○ Breaking any of the rules marked with an X will result in lost driving privileges for ___ days/weeks/months.

○ If I break a rule, I will accept the consequences *without* debating or arguing.

FOR PARENTS AND GUARDIANS

O I will drive the way I want my teen to drive.

O I will make time each week to help with extra driving practice as needed.

O I will stay calm and be patient if my teen comes to me for help.

O I will help my teen get home safely if they cannot do so.

O I will not punish my teen for the actions of their friends.

O I will ride along with my teen for _____ minutes every week to check their driving progress.

O I will provide driving tips in a patient and calm voice.

O I will meet with the driver on this date to review and update this contract: _____.

SECTION 2:

GOING SOLO: DE-STRESS YOUR FIRST TRIPS

So much info is thrown at you in driver training, including things that feel pretty random (like weird street signs that no one you know has ever seen IRL). To make your first trips less stressful, we've pulled out a few tips that will keep you safe, focused, and as calm as possible.

➤ CHAPTER 5:

Getting Settled Before You Take a Drive

Figuring out where things are and how they work can take a little time. Before you take the car out for a solo spin, give yourself a half hour to sit in the car and get to know the controls, starting with the ones mentioned in "Check It Out" on page 43.

You should also do a quick "flight check" every time you get into the car to drive it—even if you think you were the last person to use it. Taking time to double-check the position of your seat, mirrors, etc., can improve your comfort *and* your safety.

It's always a good idea to get in the car at least 15 minutes earlier than you *think* you need to leave. That way, if your "flight check" reveals any trouble (like an almost-empty gas tank), you may be able to deal with it . . . and still make it to your destination on time. Here are a few tips on what to do, why to do it, and how to do it right.

STOW YOUR STUFF SAFELY

Loose items can be a distraction if they roll around or, worse, roll underfoot. They can even become airborne if you stop suddenly. Stash heavy items (like a car jack or backpack) in the trunk. Another option for the backpack would be to secure it with a seat belt.

Small, lightweight items (like a tissue box or hoodie) can stay up front with you. But keeping most things out of reach is a good idea. It takes away the temptation to reach for something while driving.

LOCK YOUR DOORS ASAP

Some car doors lock automatically after you go over a certain speed, but don't wait for them to kick in. Lock all the doors as soon as you and any passengers are settled. Not only does this keep out unwanted "guests," it also means you won't have a door swing open while you're driving.

Don't worry about getting trapped: Most car doors also *unlock* automatically after an accident. (If they don't, you can use your vehicle escape tool to break a window—or just wait for help to arrive.)

START THE CAR AND ADJUST THE AIR

This might seem "extra," but getting enough fresh air can keep you focused (and comfortable). It can also keep you from breathing in car exhaust!

Since most heating and AC systems take a while to warm up, start the car and adjust the vents *before* you check everything else. Obviously, if you're in a garage, pull out and sit in a well-ventilated area while you sit and idle. You don't want to get carbon monoxide poisoning!

LOOK AT THE DASHBOARD FOR POSSIBLE PROBLEMS

Now that you've started the car, check the dashboard lights, using the tips from Chapter 2. Take care of any problems before you bother with the rest of this checklist. It's easy to add some air to a tire or slam the trunk shut, but if something's *really* wrong, you're not going anywhere, so there's no point in adjusting the mirrors.

Myths & Truths

MYTH: All cars are basically the same.

TRUTH: They can be more different than you might think! Even though you should always do the things in this chapter when you get in your *own* car, it's even *more* important when you're going to drive something unfamiliar. For example, if it starts to rain, you might need to flick on the wipers fast. Making sure you know how to do that—*before* you leave the driveway—can save you unnecessary stress while on the road.

SHIFT YOUR SEAT TO A COMFORTABLE SPOT

This isn't just for comfort: It can keep you safer, too. For example, if you can reach the pedals properly, you'll have better reaction time when braking. And raising up the seat if you're short can help you see through the windshield better.

Some cars have levers and others have automatic buttons. Most seats can be moved forward and back. Some allow you to adjust the height of the seat. Other will "save" the settings to the car's computer (as Driver 1 or Driver 2), so the car will reset the seat (and mirrors) at the touch of a button. Do your best with what you've got.

MAKE SURE YOUR HEADREST WILL PROTECT YOU

Many drivers (including ones with lots of experience) never bother to adjust their headrest. You should, though, because it can protect your neck better if you get rear-ended.

Luckily, it's easy to adjust: Usually you can just pull it up or push it down. The trick is getting it in the right spot. It should be 2.5 inches (or less) from the back of your head, and the middle of the headrest should be in line with the middle of your head. Think of it this way: If you were to fall back into the headrest, you want your head (not your neck) to hit it first.

FUN FACT: Some cars have headrests (and seats) that automatically adjust to protect you in a rear-end collision.

GRAB THE WHEEL AT 9 AND 3 (OR 8 AND 4)

For starters, there should be at least 10 inches between your chest and the steering wheel. (This is enough room so an airbag can inflate safely.)

If your car has a telescoping steering wheel, move it toward or away from you until it's at the right spot. (If not, you may need to readjust your seat.)

Next, place your hands where they should be while you drive—somewhere around 8 o'clock and 4 o'clock or 9 and 3 if your wheel were an analog clock. Ideally, your palms should be just below shoulder height when you grip the wheel. If they're not, see if your wheel has a "tilt" lever that can put you in a better position.

ADJUST THE MIRRORS SO YOU CAN SEE

This is easy to forget, but important to do. Your side mirrors will help you check your blind spot and your rearview mirror will help you see what's behind you. You don't want to realize that they're at the wrong angle when you're trying to change lanes!

What's the "right" angle? You should be able to look in the rearview mirror without leaning and still see the whole rear windshield (or as much as possible).

For each side mirror, angle them toward the car so that you can just barely see the side of your vehicle when you lean to look at them. Also tilt the side mirrors high enough that you'll see the vehicle behind you, not just the road.

Myths & Truths

MYTH: It's OK to hang things from the rearview mirror.

TRUTH: It's illegal to have anything blocking your view through your windshield when the car is in motion. That includes parking tags, air fresheners, charms, and pretty much everything else. In fact, the police can pull you over for it! If you need to use a hanging tag for parking at school or work, take it down before you drive.

DITCH THE DISTRACTIONS BEFORE YOU DRIVE

Set your phone on drive mode and put it away. Fix your hair and makeup now, if needed, or wait until you get to your destination. If you're wearing a hood, put it down so it won't block your side vision. Tighten the cap on your water bottle and stash it so it won't spill or roll around. You get the idea. The point is: Before you move the gear selector out of Park, make sure you'll be able to see, hear, and do whatever you need to in order to be safe. Even if you think you're great at multitasking, save those skills for when you're playing video games or watching TV.

CHECK IT OUT: WHAT TO DO THE FIRST TIME— AND EVERY TIME—YOU DRIVE

The first time you drive a different car, you'll want to take some time to learn where the most important controls are. Do this even if you're just borrowing your sister's car for one day. Ask the car's owner for a quick tutorial or look up the driver's manual online.

THE FIRST TIME YOU DRIVE A CAR, FIND THESE CONTROLS:

O Seat adjustment (up/down and forward/back)

O Mirror adjustment (rearview and side mirrors)

O Steering wheel (tilt and telescoping)

O Headlights and high beams

O Turn signals and windshield wiper (front and rear)

O Defogger (front) and defroster (rear)

O Climate control (AC and heat)

O Release levers (gas cover, trunk, and hood)

O Horn (Test it, so you know how hard you need to hit it.)

EVERY TIME YOU DRIVE A CAR, DO THESE THINGS:

O Stow your stuff safely.

O Lock your doors.

O Turn on and adjust the heat, AC, or air flow.

O Check the dashboard lights for problems.

O Adjust your seat height so you can see well out the front.

O Adjust your seat forward/back to reach the pedals easily.

O Set the headrest so its middle is even with the middle of your head.

O Make sure the headrest is no more than 2.5 inches from the back of your head.

O Set the steering wheel to 10 inches (or more) from your chest (or adjust your seat forward/back).

O Place your hands on the wheel at 9 and 3 o'clock and make sure your palms are just below shoulder height.

O Adjust your rearview mirror so you can see the whole rear windshield.

O Adjust your side mirrors so you can barely see the side of the car when you lean a little.

O Remove anything hanging from your rearview mirror.

➤ CHAPTER 6:
Good Driving Habits to "Lock In" Now

Lots of safety-related habits are second nature to seasoned drivers, and they will be for you, too . . . *eventually*. Until then, it's helpful to review some fundamentals from driver's ed. These include things like scanning the road, maintaining a safe distance, watching your speed, knowing who goes first at intersections, and what to do before a left-hand turn.

SCAN THE ROAD—AND NOT JUST IN THE FRONT

It's important to be aware of *all* of your surroundings at *all* times. This helps you spot problems as soon as possible, which gives you more time to deal with them—as much as 15 seconds more.

Don't just stare straight ahead, though. Set your gaze "down the road" about a quarter mile (or a city block), and keep an eye on everything between you and that point.

Also glance in the side mirrors to get the big picture. Just make it quick! You don't want to rear-end someone because you were staring too long at the Tesla in the next lane.

Keep an eye on what's behind you, too. For example, if you're slowing down, glance in the rearview mirror to see if the driver behind you is slowing down, too. If not, you can put on your hazard lights to get their attention—or you can get out of their way.

In fact, you should *always* have an "escape route" in mind, whether you're moving or stopped. Leaving enough space between you and the person in front of you will allow you more time to avoid an unexpected problem.

REMEMBER: "ONLY A FOOL BREAKS THE 2-SECOND RULE"

This is a favorite saying of driving instructors all over the world. It's a good way to remember that you should always maintain a safe following distance from the car in front of you. Doing this means you'll have some time—at least 2 seconds— to react if they make a mistake or hit the brakes.

At slower speeds, experts say to use the 2-second rule to gauge your distance. As the vehicle ahead passes a stationary object (like a tree), simply count "1 one-thousand, 2 one-thousand." OR just say "Only a fool breaks the 2-second rule," which (fun fact) takes 2 seconds to say!

Your vehicle should not pass the same object before you finish that count. If it does, ease off a bit. If you're on a faster road, use the 4-second rule. If weather's bad, make it 8 seconds, and if the road is slippery, leave a good 20 seconds between you and the vehicle ahead.

Maintaining a safe distance can be tough if there's a lot of traffic because other cars may see this as an "opening" and scoot in front of you. If that happens, just ease off again to gain some more distance, or wait a bit to see if they speed up and create some distance themselves.

Stop-and-go traffic in cities can also make it tough to leave very much space, so just do your best. There, keep it shorter than a car length (or someone else will slide in).

Keep in mind, of course, that these are just guidelines, and you'll have to let common sense and good judgment guide your actual decisions.

STAY VISIBLE—BY AVOIDING BLIND SPOTS

Don't forget to keep some space on your *sides*, too, especially when driving on a multilane road. This can help you avoid being in another driver's blind spot.

Basically, the blind spot is any area that the driver can't see without turning their head. It's usually worst on the rear passenger side of the vehicle because you can't see that even if you use your side mirror.

Tractor trailer drivers have even bigger blind spots. Theirs are right in front of the cab, right behind the truck, and on both sides of the trailer where it attaches to the cab. Adjust your speed (within the speed limit) to get out of these blind spots.

TIP: Vehicles aren't the only thing that can be in your blind spots. Pedestrians sometimes wind up there, too. That's why you need to keep scanning constantly.

WATCH YOUR SPEED—AND EVERYONE ELSE'S

Speed limits are chosen by transportation experts based on studies that include how much traffic there is, what the road is made of, where it's located, and other factors. Basically, they have done the math for you, so you know that's the safest upper limit. (It's also the law, and you don't want a speeding ticket!)

Of course, you may need to drive *below* the speed limit at times, such as in bad weather. But try not to drive slower than the flow of traffic, either.

The best way to avoid an accident is to maintain a speed that's similar to the vehicles around you but within the posted speed limit. If you feel like you can't drive 65 miles per hour, stick to side roads. If you can't stick with the flow of traffic in bad weather, maybe it's time to pull off and get a coffee until it clears up.

Stats & Facts

STAT: You burn about 5% more gas for every 5 miles per hour above 60 miles per hour.

FACT: Sticking to the speed limit saves gas (which saves you money). If your car has an "ECO" setting, use it: It will automatically make adjustments that save even *more* fuel while you drive.

USE YOUR TURN SIGNAL—EVERY TIME

Sometimes you won't realize a person is nearby—on foot, on a bike, or in a vehicle—until the last second. That's why you should *always* use your turn signal before you make a turn or change lanes.

After making the turn, make sure your signal turns *off*. Even though it will usually do that automatically, it may not if you didn't turn at a sharp angle, such as when "bearing" right or left.

UNDERSTAND INTERSECTIONS—BUT BE FLEXIBLE

First, never assume the other drivers are going to stop at an intersection. Make sure they do *before* you take your turn. Second, make sure that you come to a full stop, even if no one else is around. (Doing things every time will help make it a habit—and maybe keep you from getting a traffic ticket.) Third, don't try to sneak around a stopped vehicle or turn quickly to beat the light at a traffic stop.

Pretty much anything that involves being quick, sneaky, or surprising should be left to the Hollywood stunt drivers.

Now for the tough part: If you reach an intersection at the same time as another vehicle, the person on the *right* has the *right*-of-way. But, as with every other situation on the road, safety is more important than being "right." So, if another driver seems bent on going first, just let them.

LOOK LEFT-RIGHT-LEFT—BUT WAIT UNTIL IT'S SAFE

Some new drivers will avoid making left turns onto busy roads. That's not a bad idea if the thought scares you. You *never* want to pull out into traffic if you're not sure you can do it safely. Plus, it's tough for new drivers to judge other drivers' speed and distance. So know that finding another route is a perfectly acceptable option.

When you *are* going to make a left turn, look left . . . then right . . . then left again. Only "go" if it's still safe. If not, repeat the process until you can make the turn with plenty of time to spare. Don't worry if someone behind you is honking. Being safe is worth the wait.

CHECK IT OUT: TROUBLE AHEAD, TROUBLE BEHIND

Here are a few things you should be watching for when scanning the road. Use all of your mirrors, windows, and windshields, and know when you need to glance over your shoulder to check your blind spot. (It's a lot, we know.) Some things to watch for include:

VEHICLES & PEOPLE

- O Vehicles and people entering/exiting the road
- O Vehicles changing lanes
- O Vehicles slowing down or stopping in front of you
- O Drivers who are behaving strangely (weaving, for example)
- O Accidents, breakdowns, and debris
- O Construction zones and equipment
- O Oversize vehicles or vehicles transporting items that could come loose

SIGNS & SIGNALS

- O Brake lights
- O Turn signals
- O Hazard lights
- O Road signs
- O Traffic signals
- O Railroad crossings
- O Directional signs
- O Warning signs and signals

➤ CHAPTER 7:
Reduce the Stress of Your First Solo Trips

It's "all you" now: No parental passenger to point out hazards. No driving instructor with their foot hovering over that weird passenger-side brake pedal. Still, you want to show them you know what you're doing. That means making sure you don't run into any trouble, especially on your first trips.

The best way to do that is to avoid anything that might cause a problem. Smooth the way for yourself, and you'll be able to report to your parents that your trip went completely fine (and not have your nose grow like Pinocchio's).

CHECK THE WEATHER ON A WEBSITE OR APP

Before you grab the keys, check the local weather. If the forecast is nasty, ask an adult to drive you that day—or at least to ride along so they can coach you through it.

If your parents are willing, you might be able to drive yourself to your destination (while the skies are clear), then have them pick you up later if needed. Also check out the tips in Chapter 18 on how to drive in bad weather if you *can't* avoid it.

Myths & Truths

MYTH: If you got your license, you're ready to drive solo.

TRUTH: Maybe and maybe not. Even if you did everything correctly in the tests, it's normal to be nervous about driving on your own. Some people are *extra stressed*—for example, people who were in a car accident or who have a phobia or anxiety disorder.

If you're in that group, conquering your fear is possible—and important for your safety. And it's important that you not drive alone if you're super-anxious.

Don't think you're alone: A lot of people are learning to drive later. In fact, only about 61% of 18-year-olds had their drivers' license in 2018.

You may just need a few extra weeks (or months) of driving with an adult in the car. Or you may want to take some extra driving lessons. You may also want to ask your pediatrician or other doctor about cognitive behavioral therapy. This is where you meet with someone who can give you specific strategies to calm your nerves before you drive.

USE GPS TO FIGURE OUT WHEN TO LEAVE

Many of us have heard this from coaches and teachers: "If you're *early*, you're on time, and if you're on time, you're *late*." Their point, of course, is that you shouldn't plan to arrive at your destination at the last minute. It makes a bad impression, and it can make you more stressed while you're driving there.

Chances are you don't know how long it will take to get to most places. A simple way to find out? Plug in your current location and your destination on a GPS app, and let it calculate your estimated travel time.

If you do this a day or so beforehand, be sure to try it *again* about half an hour before you actually plan to leave. Traffic patterns may have changed by then. Lucky for you, GPS devices "know" if there's an accident or slowdown, and they'll recalculate your estimated arrival time for you.

Running late? Here's another motto to remember, and it cancels out the other one if you're running late already: "It's better to arrive late than not at all." Harsh, but true. And nothing you could do (including speeding) would make much of a difference anyway.

DRIVE ONLY WHEN THE LIGHTING IS RIGHT

At night, it gets harder to see and everything looks different. You need to remember extra stuff like turning on headlights and high beams. You might be more tired after a full day of school. And most of the fatal teen crashes happen between 9 p.m. and midnight. You get the picture. At least for now, stick to driving in daylight.

That said, certain times of day can be tough, too. When the sun is rising or setting, you can wind up with a lot of glare on the windshield, which makes it tougher for everyone to see (not just you). If you *must* drive at those times, use your visor, wear polarized sunglasses, and turn on your headlights so other drivers can see you better. Also, slow down and leave extra distance between you and the car ahead. Keeping your windshield and eyeglasses clean can also help prevent glare during the day and at night.

STICK TO ROUTES THAT ARE FAMILIAR

Though GPS can help you go just about anywhere, it's just another distraction, which you definitely don't need.

Before you take your first drive by yourself, choose a nearby location that you would like to drive to alone someday, such as your job or your practice field. Make sure it's not very far away and doesn't require driving on a highway or managing risky intersections or tough turns.

Next, ask an adult to help you map out the easiest route possible, then drive that exact route repeatedly with them beside you. (This may not be the *fastest* route, but safety is more important.) When you think it's locked in your memory, test yourself by asking that adult to pretend they don't know the way, so you have to tell them where to turn. If you can do that, you're likely ready to do it alone.

Start with just one or two routes, then ask about adding more when you're totally comfortable with those.

GO IT ALONE FOR A WHILE (THAT MEANS NO PASSENGERS!)

Your parents may be excited for you to take over chauffeur duties, but siblings can be some of the most distracting passengers of all. Your friends may not be much better, especially the ones who are a little loud or wild. Saying No to *all* passengers also can help you avoid friend drama because you don't have to pick and choose who you'll take where and when. Many states won't even *allow* new drivers have peers or younger passengers in the car until they've logged a certain number of miles. (Check with your state's Department of Transportation to find out.)

Your furry friends can also be bad company in the car. Pets can get underfoot (literally) if they're not seat-belted or crated, and they can make a lot of noise!

TRUST US: Once you begin taking on passengers later, you may miss the peace and quiet of solo drives.

Stats & Facts

STAT: Only 15% of teens think their friends are inexperienced drivers.

FACT: Don't be overconfident in how well you or your friends drive. It's not possible to be great at something right away. (Think of when you tried a new sport or hobby. You messed up plenty.) So know, in your heart, that you're a newbie, and focus your full attention on the road.

Q&A: Ask Yourself

☐ During my last drive, did anything startle or stress me?

☐ Did I see a sign or signal that I didn't understand?

☐ Was there any part of my route that was confusing or too challenging?

☐ Do I want to tell my parents or instructor about something that went really well or a decision I'm proud of?

Q&A: Ask Someone Else

☐ *If a problem happened:* What should I do if this happens again?

☐ *If you saw (and avoided) a potential problem:* Did I do the right thing? What can I do better next time?

☐ *If the route was too challenging:* Is there an easier, safer route to this destination? If not, can we drive this route together again, so I can get some tips?

CHECK IT OUT: THE NHTSA'S "5 TO DRIVE" RULES

The National Highway Traffic Safety Administration (NHTSA) recommends that teens follow these rules when they hit the road. Some of them are covered in other chapters, and some are covered here. They're *all* really easy to remember. (Your parents should follow them, too, except for #2—though that's probably on their wish list.)

1. No cell phones while driving
2. No extra passengers
3. No speeding
4. No alcohol (or anything that dulls the senses)
5. No driving or riding without a seat belt

➤ CHAPTER 8:

Fueling Up: Tips for Gas Stations (and Drive-Throughs)

Pulling up to a gas pump or drive-through window can be tricky: Sometimes it involves a tight turn, tight squeeze, or other unexpected challenges. That's why it's a good idea to tackle them with a parent or driving instructor at first.

At the end of this chapter, you'll find some questions to help you decide whether to give a drive-through a try by yourself. Also check out the play-by-play guide for refueling, which lists the steps. (There are a lot of them, but they're all pretty easy to do.)

The rest of this chapter is dedicated to the little tips and tricks that your instructors may have forgotten about—and that can make the experience easier (and safer, too).

LEARN THE ABCS OF FUEL GRADES

There are two types of fuel: *gas* and *diesel*. Make sure you
know which your car takes. (It's usually marked on the gas
cap, if you forget.) Using the wrong kind of fuel can cause
real problems.

There are three grades of gas to choose from: *regular*,
mid-grade, and *premium*. Most sedan and compact cars run
fine on regular (which is also the cheapest). But check the
owner's manual and/or ask the owner. (Some people use regular
gas, even when the manual suggests a higher grade, and vice versa.)

If you see the words "ethanol" or "biodiesel," the gas or diesel has been mixed
with plant-based fuels or recycled grease (like from restaurant fryers). These
ingredients help reduce the use of petroleum products, which is good for the
planet, and they burn cleaner, which is good for your car, too.

Of course, cars that run on electricity are becoming more popular, too.
Some of them are battery-powered only, but others have both a gas engine and
an electric engine. There are versions that plug into an outlet and some with
batteries that self-charge as you drive. If you're responsible for this kind of car,
you'll want to spend some time learning about your specific model. Try the
videos on the manufacturer's website to get started.

REMEMBER THESE TRICKS FOR FINDING THE GAS TANK

It's easy to forget which *side* the gas tank is on. Luckily, most cars have a little
arrow or triangle near the gas gauge on the dashboard. (It's next to the picture
of a gas pump.) If not, you can write a reminder on a sticky note and put it on the
dashboard or console.

Another tricky part of getting ready to fill the tank? Opening the gas tank
cover! Sometimes there's a lever inside the car (usually on the driver's side near
the door). Other times, there isn't a lever at all. If that's the case, try pushing on
one edge of the gas-cap cover, and it will pop open on its own.

LOCK IT UP, BUT DON'T LOCK YOURSELF OUT

Don't unlock your doors as soon as you're parked alongside the pump. Instead, shut off the vehicle, turn off your lights, put the car in Park, and get out your credit card or cash. Also check out your surroundings, and if you see something that feels shady, go to a different station.

Also take your keys, phone, and money with you when you get out of the car—then lock the doors again. Having your keys will prevent a lockout, and locking the doors can prevent theft.

Myths & Truths

MYTH: Using a cell phone near a gas pump can start a fire.

TRUTH: There's no evidence that this has ever happened in the history of ever. Which is why you'll now see many gas stations allowing you to pay using an app on your phone! This is convenient and it can save you money, too. Even so, don't play on your phone while you wait for the tank to fill. It's best to stay aware of what's going on around you.

WAIT UNTIL THE LAST MINUTE TO UNSCREW THE GAS CAP

As soon as you unscrew the gas cap, it starts to leak gas vapor into the air (not good for you or the planet). This is why you should never smoke at a gas station. You also shouldn't get in and out of the car while the gas cap is unscrewed, as this can cause a spark from static electricity that could ignite the vapor.

DO SOME "LIGHT" CLEANING WHILE YOU WAIT

Many pump handles have a locking lever that holds the trigger for you while the gas is flowing. This gives you some time to wash your windshield with the squeegee and fluid provided by the gas station. Want to go the extra mile? Clean your headlights and taillights, too. Believe it or not, built-up dirt can block the glow of headlights by up to 50%. That's why experts suggest washing them at least once a week.

Myths & Truths

MYTH: It's smart to "top off" the gas tank.

TRUTH: Pumps are designed to shut off automatically when your tank is at the correct fullness. Squeezing in just a little bit more can cause problems with your car. There's a vapor-sensing device inside the tank, and that extra gas can mess it up.

Also avoid tapping the nozzle inside the tank before you pull it out. That can damage both the nozzle and your car. Instead, when you remove the nozzle, quickly point it up to the sky, keeping it clear of your car and clothes as you holster it.

TURN THE CAP UNTIL YOU HEAR THREE CLICKS

A loose fuel cap can make your "check engine" light come on, which can make your heart rate skyrocket. So, make sure you replace the gas cap properly *every time*. On most cars, that means turning it "three clicks" to the right. If yours doesn't click, just turn it until you feel a hard stop.

GO PAPERLESS WHENEVER POSSIBLE

The display on the gas pumps will likely ask if you want a printed receipt. Unless your parents ask you for copies, it's best to choose "No." Millions of trees are cut down each year to make paper receipts for America alone. Every time you opt out, you're making a little bit of difference. Plus, studies have found that many receipts are coated with chemicals that can pose a health risk if absorbed by the body.

If you want a record of the transaction, use your smartphone to take a photo of the pump or refer to your online billing statement when you pay by card.

Q&A: Ask Yourself
(Drive-Through Edition)

Before you decide to go through a drive-through, whether it's at a fast-food chain, bank, pharmacy, or car wash, ask yourself these questions. If the answer is no, just park in the lot and go inside instead—or head to a different location that is easier to access. Do this until you've gotten better at maneuvering the car in tight spots.

☐ Do I know how to get to the drive-through lane? Is it clearly marked?

☐ Does the drive-through access require me to make a sharp turn or does it look like a tight squeeze?

☐ Is the drive-through really busy? Will I be able to get in line without being in an unsafe spot to stop?

☐ Is there a real reason I need to use a drive-through?

NOTE: Automated car washes usually have a worker to help you steer your wheels into the tracks that will pull you through. They will also remind you to put the car in Park or Neutral and take your foot off the brake. Always follow the signs and instructions, and you'll come out squeaky clean.

Q&A: Ask Someone Else
(Gas Station Edition)

☐ What kind of fuel should I put in this car? Gas or diesel? Regular, medium, or premium grade?

☐ Where do you like to get gas? What do you like about that gas station?

☐ Should I use a "rewards" card or app to save money on gas?

CHECK IT OUT: A STEP-BY-STEP GUIDE TO PUMPING GAS

Refilling your tank isn't exactly hard, but there are a lot of steps! Here's the quick rundown, in case you're afraid you'll forget something.

1. PULL UP TO A PUMP

O Pull into the fuel station.

O Pull alongside an empty pump.

O Make sure the fuel pump nozzle will be able to reach the gas tank.

O If needed, move to another pump or pull the car closer.

2. SHUT DOWN EVERYTHING

O Turn off the car. Put it in Park.

O Turn off anything that uses the battery (lights, radio, etc.)

3. GET YOUR MONEY AND GET OUT OF THE CAR

O Grab your keys and whatever you're using to pay (cash, card, or cell phone).

O Pop the gas-cap cover using the release lever if there is one.

O Get out and lock the car doors.

4. PICK YOUR WAY TO PAY

O If you're paying with a card or your phone, follow the directions on the pump.

O If you're paying with cash, go inside and prepay.

5. PREPARE TO PUMP

O Select the fuel grade.

O Pop the gas-cap cover, if needed.

O Unscrew the gas cap.

O Lift the handle from its holster. (Don't pull the trigger yet!)

O Insert the nozzle into the gas tank.

6. PUMP THE GAS

O Pull the trigger (to start gas flowing).

O Lock open the trigger if you can.

O Wash the windows and headlights.

O Listen for the click.

O If you're holding the trigger, let go when you hear the click.

7. REVERSE THE PROCESS

O Remove the nozzle.

O Return the nozzle to the holster.

O Tighten the gas cap (until it clicks 3 times or stops).

O Close the gas-cap cover.

O If you paid cash, go back inside for change if the pump kicked off before reaching the prepaid amount.

O If you chose to print a receipt, take it with you.

8. GET SETTLED AGAIN

O Get in the car.

O Lock your doors.

O Fasten your seat belt.

O Put away your money and cards.

O Take a breath.

O Double-check you've done everything in step 7 before you start the car and pull away.

➤ CHAPTER 9:
Parking Pointers for All Kinds of Spaces

We won't lie: Parallel parking *isn't* easy! That's why there's a step-by-step guide to it at the end of this chapter.

Still, that doesn't mean that *other* parking situations are super simple. Ask an adult to help you practice parking in all kinds of places: parking lots, garages, and anywhere else you're likely to go. Also keep these tips in mind when parking the car by yourself.

STAY INSIDE THE PAINTED LINES

It's OK to *color* outside the lines, but when you're driving in a parking lot, pay attention to the aisle markings, even if the lot is really empty. To be more exact, *don't* go driving across the aisles horizontally. Many accidents happen that way. Plus, it can make other drivers angry. In general, you only want your car to be somewhere that a car *should* be, so you won't surprise or confuse other drivers. Yes, that means you don't cut through the grocery store parking lot to get to the video game store faster. (There's no respawning IRL.)

PICK THE BEST SPACE POSSIBLE

Look for an empty space with no (or few) cars nearby and away from parking-lot traffic. Don't park in the first few spaces at the end of a row, where other drivers will be entering and exiting. Also avoid parking near carts, which could roll into your car and leave a dent. If it's nighttime, look for a space near a light (and other cars and people), for safety's sake.

Once you find the "perfect" spot, though, remember it's not worth fighting for. If another driver wants it badly, just let them have it. Road rage isn't only a problem on the road!

PARK ONLY WHERE YOU'RE ALLOWED TO

There are lots of places you're *allowed* to park, and lots of places you're *not*. Even if a friend tells you they "never" get a ticket in a certain place, don't take a chance if it says "No Parking." (Your driver's manual should list what's off-limits in your state.)

FUN FACT: Sometimes the markings on the street or signs will be different than the law. For instance, you usually aren't supposed to park within 15 feet of a fire hydrant, but sometimes local authorities will allow you to park closer. If so, the painted curb and signs will tell you what's off-limits.

Myths & Truths

MYTH: It's OK to park on the "wrong" side of a quiet street.

TRUTH: When you're parked on *any* type of roadway, you need to be facing the same direction as traffic is flowing in the lane that's beside you. Parking on the *other* side of the street is illegal, no matter where you are or how little traffic there is around you.

Why? For starters, you'd need to drive on the wrong side of the street (into oncoming traffic) to get there, which is also illegal. Second, you could wind up with a parking ticket. Third, it can be tougher to see when you need to pull out, especially if someone parks in "front" of you.

POSITION YOURSELF TO PARK

In a parking lot, this means waiting until both driving aisles are empty and nothing is coming. Position your car as far to the side as you can safely so you have plenty of room to turn. Don't start to turn until you're halfway past the parking space in *front* of the spot you're aiming for.

Remember to keep looking all around you the whole time, using your mirrors and turning your head as needed. If you run into trouble, stop and reset—or find a different space that's an easier fit.

CHECK IF YOU'RE CENTERED

Wherever you park, make sure your car is centered between the lines and that there is enough room to open the car doors on either side of you. It may take a few tries to get your placement just right, but that's better than blocking some-one else from getting back into their car!

Also make sure you're centered from front to back, so both bumpers are inside the space. You don't want to be sticking out into traffic or into another person's parking space.

MAKE SURE YOUR CAR WILL STAY PUT

After you're satisfied with your parking job, put the car in Park and *always* put on the emergency brake, even on flat ground. If you're on a hill, you'll have to do one more thing: Turn your front tires at an angle. Here's the rule:

- If you're going to park facing UPHILL on a TWO-WAY STREET with a CURB, park with your front tires turned completely to the LEFT.

- On any other type of hill, turn your front tires completely to the RIGHT when you park.

USE AN APP TO MARK WHERE YOU PARKED

This is a trick your parents might not know: You can use a map app to remember the location of your car. On Google Maps, you just open the app, tap on the blue dot, and choose "Set as parking location" from the pop-up menu. Then close the app (to save your battery). Your location will still be saved when you open it again. Other map apps also offer this feature.

ANOTHER OPTION: Use your phone to snap a photo of a street sign or landmark that is near your parking spot. No cell service? Look for where your parking aisle comes to a T with the building and walk back to the car starting at that location.

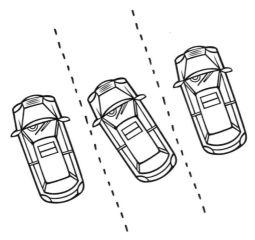

Myths & Truths

MYTH: It's always legal to back into—or pull through—an empty space in a parking lot.

TRUTH: *Both* of these moves are illegal in some states. If the pull-through move is *not* illegal where you live, don't try it unless you can clearly see that nothing is coming from either direction in the other aisle. You don't want to come nose-to-nose with another car that's parking. Also, don't pull through if the parking lot has diagonal spaces, which is basically impossible without driving over the lines. (That's never a good move.)

MAINTAIN AWARENESS WHILE WALKING

As you exit the car and walk to your destination, keep an eye out for vehicles, pedestrians, and potential hazards. Watch for cars that are looking to pull out or pull into a space. Don't walk through or stand in an empty space, either—someone might be aiming for it and not expect you to be there.

HAVE A SOLID EXIT STRATEGY

In some states, it's illegal to pull through! (See Myths & Truths.) Other times, you won't be able to because a car's ahead of you.

If you must back out of a parking space, first look at the cars on either side of you to see which is closest to your car. If you're able to, back out toward the closer car because there will be more room for the nose of your car as you exit.

Put your car in Reverse a few seconds before you're ready to go: That turns on your back-up lights, so people will know what you're planning. Wait until the coast is completely clear before you pull out. Remember to watch for adults, kids, electric carts, strollers, and other things—not just other vehicles.

BE PREPARED TO PAY FOR PARKING

Parking garages, parking meters, and valet parking all cost money. In many cases, you can pay with your smartphone. Other times, you can use cash, coins, or a card. (You might want to ask your parents for an emergency credit card to use in cases where the meter doesn't take coins or cash.) If you use valet parking (unlikely, we know), give the valet a cash tip of $2 to $5 when they return your car to you. If you're heading to a city, do some research first to find a parking garage or pay-to-park lot that's near where you're headed. Sometimes there are even coupons available online. (Paying to park in a city usually isn't cheap!)

CHECK IT OUT: A STEP-BY-STEP GUIDE TO PARALLEL PARKING

We'd like to start by thanking whoever came up with the idea of self-parking cars, and we hope it's standard in all cars someday. Now, though, if you don't have an auto-park option in your vehicle, you'll have to take matters into your own hands.

There's no shame in avoiding parallel parking until you feel really comfortable with it by practicing with cones or trash cans at home (with an adult in the car to guide you). One survey of drivers reported that 45% weren't confident in their parallel parking skills—and not all of them were as new to it as you.

Below, you'll find a simplified breakdown of the basic steps to parallel parking. It can help jog your memory if you don't do this task often.

In these directions, we're going to assume that you will choose a legal parking space that's 3 to 5 feet longer than your car—and that you'll be constantly using your mirrors and turning your head to take in your surroundings. Of course, you won't move your car unless the coast is clear, and when you do move, you'll take it slow. You know all that, but it's like when your mom tells you to be careful: We just had to say it.

○ Put on your **right turn signal** *before* you reach the space.

○ Pull up **parallel to the car parked in front** of the empty space. (We'll call this "Car A," and we'll call the car behind "your" space "Car B.") Leave 2 to 3 feet between the sides of your cars.

○ Stop, look all around you, and when it's safe, **start backing up straight**.

○ When **the middle of your car** is even with **the rear bumper of Car A**, turn the steering wheel all the way to the **RIGHT**. Stop when the headlights of the car behind you (Car B) are in your driver's side mirror.

○ When **your right-side mirror lines up with Car A's rear bumper**, turn your steering wheel to the **LEFT**.

○ Check your position: You should be **12 inches or less from the curb** and **centered between Car A and Car B**.

○ There are lots of videos online that show what this process looks like in real life, which may make it easier to understand (and remember).

A final thought: Driving is one activity where winners sometimes quit: If at any point you feel that you can't manage to park in the spot you chose, it's OK (and smart) to abandon the effort. Stop the car, take a breath, and just go find a *different* space. No harm, no foul, and no dented bumper.

➤ CHAPTER 10:
Along for the Ride: Avoid Problems with Passengers

Before you learned to drive, you probably didn't think much about how to be a good passenger. Now, though, you probably understand why your parents used to tell you to quiet down in the backseat. If wild passengers are distracting for adults, of course they cause problems for new drivers, too.

It's easier to keep things under control if you explain the ground rules to your passengers ahead of time. You can always blame the law (or your parents or driving instructor) if your friends roll their eyes when you tell them to buckle up or calm down. Here's what to know when inviting other people along for the ride.

MAKE SURE IT'S LEGAL

Depending on the level of driver's license you have, you might not be legally allowed to carry any passengers under the age of 18 unless an adult is with you. You probably know if your state has a Graduated Driver Licensing (GDL) law, but if you're not sure what that means, you can find a link to them on the website for the Governors Highway Safety Association (ghsa. org/state-laws/states).

Surprisingly, a few states don't have a GDL law. You can still benefit from them, though. Use what other states are doing to keep yourself safe. For example, GDL laws usually recommend that in the first 12 months after they get a license, teen drivers have no same-age passengers and that they have no more than two passengers until they turn 18.

Stats & Facts

STAT: Teen drivers are 2.5 times more likely to do something risky when another teen is on board.

FACT: Every added teenage passenger raises the risk even more. Keep this in mind when you're a driver (*and* when you're a passenger), especially if you have a tough time saying no to peer pressure.

MAKE SURE YOU'RE READY

Does peer pressure get to you? Answer honestly on this one. If so, you may be better off driving alone. Also ask yourself what your friends are like. Are they quiet or wild or somewhere in between? Consider where you'd be driving if you picked them up. Would you have to take a highway or driver farther than you're comfortable with now? Have you had a little fender bender or a "scare" on the road? You may prefer to say no to *all* passengers for now. If you do decide to pick and choose based on driving distance, personality, and other factors, just be careful: Feelings can easily get hurt, and you don't need the drama. You'll probably "feel" ready for company at some point, and when you do, you can ask your parents and driving instructor if they agree.

MAKE SURE IT'S SAFE

Different states have different seat-belt laws. While seat belts are usually required at least in the front seats, it varies who pays the ticket if a passenger isn't buckled up. Sometimes it's the driver and sometimes it's the passenger. A seat-belt ticket can make insurance rates go up, too.

Of course, those aren't the most important reasons to buckle up, but they may help convince unruly friends. (And if they give you a hard time with this, they're probably not going to follow your other car rules either.) You may not want to think about this, but in 2016 almost 60% of the deaths in teen-driver crashes were people who didn't buckle up. You don't want to have a friend's injury on your conscience.

Also remember that smaller passengers can be hurt if an airbag deploys, so anyone under age 13 should ride in the back seat. And if you're driving siblings who need a car seat or booster, make sure you understand how they work and how to double-check that they're secure.

Myths & Truths

MYTH: Passengers don't need to pay attention to the road.

TRUTH: When you're a passenger, keep your eyes on traffic, too, especially if you're riding with a driver who doesn't have much experience. If you're in charge of watching the GPS, don't freak out if the driver misses a turn (or is about to). As long as what the driver is doing is not unsafe or illegal, just let them finish their turn (or whatever) and look for a place where they can turn around and get back on track. Ideally, though, you'll look ahead on the map a little bit so you can give the driver some warning of where and when the next turn will be.

Also watch for safe (and unsafe) driving. The driver should stay within the speed limit, not make risky moves, have both hands on the wheel, and not be doing anything distracting like eating, drinking, smoking, vaping, or using their phone. (See Chapter 24 for other times people shouldn't be driving.)

If the driver is doing something unsafe and won't stop, make an excuse to stop at the next open restaurant or busy store. (For example, say you need a restroom.) Get out, call your parents for a ride, and don't get back into the friend's car while you wait. (Of course, use the restroom, too, if you need to.)

- -

MAKE SURE CONDITIONS ARE PERFECT

Don't drive with passengers in bad weather, at night, on highways or unfamiliar roads, or when anything else is out of your comfort zone. You probably shouldn't be doing these things anyway for the first few weeks or months of driving by yourself. When you do try driving in these conditions without an adult, do it alone so you're better able to focus.

MAKE SURE ADULTS STAY CALM, TOO

The people who taught you how to drive may have trouble easing up on the advice. Even if they're cool about it, other adults may be nervous the first time they ride with you because they don't know your skills. It's OK to let them know when they are distracting you or making you nervous. (That's clearly not their goal!) You might want to suggest they talk to your driving instructor, who can reassure them (or not!) about your abilities. Or maybe you will agree that your mom or dad won't be a passenger for a while. If you really do need more training, go for it. You can tell the driving instructor you'd like some more advanced lessons, along with the things you want to work on most.

CHECK IT OUT: SETTING THE RULES FOR PASSENGERS

To come up with the rules for your riders, sit down with your parents and talk about what is important to them (and you). Here are a few rules you may want to adopt for your passengers—and when you're in the passenger seat yourself.

GOOD RULES FOR EVERYONE

○ Always wear your seat belt when the car is moving.

○ Don't bring anything illegal into the car. (That includes drugs, alcohol, cigarettes, or vaping devices.)

○ Don't pressure the driver to do anything risky or illegal.

○ Don't be loud, wild, or distracting.

○ While you're still parked, ask the driver if there's anything you can do to be helpful.

OTHER QUESTIONS TO CONSIDER

○ Are passengers allowed to eat or drink in the car?

○ Is it OK for passengers to have music on, talk to each other, or be on their phones?

○ Are there any pet peeves you or your parents have that riders may not know?

SECTION 3:

GOING THE EXTRA MILE: WHAT TO EXPECT, WHEREVER YOU GO

Once you start to expand your driving beyond school, home, work, and after-school practices, you'll quickly see that every new route has different challenges to tackle and bosses to beat. Driving on unfamiliar roads means you need to pay attention to extras like directions and GPS devices. You'll also come across scenarios you may not be used to—like a horse and buggy in the country and one-way streets in the city. Scoping out the possibilities now, on paper, can give you an edge when you face them for real.

➤ CHAPTER 11:

Finding Your Way: Directions, Detours, and More

After you've mastered a few familiar routes, you'll probably want to start picking up friends at their houses, driving yourself to school events, or going out for nachos on Trivia Night. Within a few years, who knows? You'll probably be all over the map. Right now, though, you'll need to practice how to get from point A to point B.

Knowing that North West is the name of Kim Kardashian and Kanye West's first child won't get you anywhere. But remembering that West is to the *left* on a compass can be helpful. So can the tips in this chapter.

PRETEND YOU'RE A SURVIVOR CONTESTANT

The show *Survivor* may be one of the only places you've
seen anyone use a paper map recently. But driving experts
recommend that you have a map or road atlas in your glove
box at all times. Sometimes WiFi isn't available or phone batteries die, or an app
map's error can dump you in a cornfield instead of at the mall. A paper map is a
good Plan B in all those situations.

You might be able to get some free maps of your state or local area from
your driving school, the DMV, or city tourism office. Auto clubs and even some
supermarkets carry them, too.

PRACTICE TIP: Get a paper map, find your house, then pick a favorite spot
like a fro-yo shop. Trace a few different routes you could take to get there, using
a different color highlighter for each one. Doing this can be a real eye-opener.
Things are often closer (or farther) than we realize.

Myths & Truths

MYTH: GPS won't steer you wrong.

TRUTH: GPS signals can bounce off or get blocked by things in the atmosphere
or on the ground, like bridges, buildings, and trees. Tunnels that go underground,
under water, or through a mountain can cause a dropped signal, too.

Other times, though, the app isn't up to date. To see if that's the problem,
pull over and open up a *different* map app. If the new app is OK, you might want
to report the problem when you get home. Simply go onto the map app's
website and search for their "report an issue" page. Your report could save
future drivers from getting lost.

LEARN THE LANGUAGE OF DRIVING APPS

Every GPS program looks, sounds, and works a little bit differently. The program usually has you type in your start and end points, then shows you the "best" route (usually the fastest or most direct). Some give you a few route options to choose from. You'll also see how long the trip will take in current traffic. (Keep in mind that the app won't know that it takes 30 minutes to get out of the high school parking lot.) Most of these programs also have advanced settings that let you narrow down choices—like avoiding routes with highways and toll roads. Some even let you print out the script (like "Turn right onto Snowdrift Road"), which is helpful if you learn best by reading on paper.

PRACTICE TIP: Research driving-directions websites and apps and pick one you like or ask friends or adults for a suggestion. Then have an adult drive you somewhere (like the high school) and follow along with the app. That way, you can get used to how they deliver directions (like "In X feet, turn right onto Y Street"). It can also help you see how much warning you'll get before you need to turn.

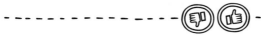

Myths & Truths

MYTH: It's OK to hold your phone if you're just using the GPS.

TRUTH: It's *always* illegal to hold your phone in your hand *even if you're just using it for directions!*

Holding a phone counts as "distracted driving"—which makes sense because your eyes aren't on the road and at least one of your hands is not on the wheel. Having your phone at your fingertips also makes it more tempting to "just check this one text" or whatever. Which obviously is a bad move.

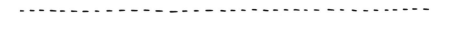

CHECK THE GPS LAWS IN YOUR STATE

Tech gurus gave us GPS, but the safety gurus said, "Not so fast!" Just because GPS is available doesn't mean it's always legal. Different states have different laws. Some states only allow the use of a built-in navigation system (one that's part of the car). Some let you use a GPS app on your phone, but the phone must be in a docking station. And those states often have laws about where you can *mount* the docking station.

Many states won't let drivers under 18 use a phone at all—*even in hands-free mode*—when driving. The great thing about GPS is that it will tell you about upcoming moves way in advance—like when to turn or when to change lanes. This can actually make you safer when you can't see very well, like at night or in bad weather, which you'll have to drive in at some point.

PRACTICE TIP: Check your state's DMV website for GPS laws. Or ask your driving instructor or another adult for help getting the official info.

LET A PASSENGER TAKE THE ROLE OF "NAVIGATOR"

As a new driver, you may be tempted to glance at the GPS screen more often, just because of nerves. You can avoid that by choosing a passenger to be in charge of looking at the map app or written directions.

PRACTICE TIP: Make sure the person you pick can be trusted to stay calm and focused the whole time. Also remind them to warn you about the next move way before you need to know. And they have to promise not to freak if you mess up and miss a turn. (Or, like, ever. You don't need that drama.)

Stats & Facts

STAT: A 2-second glance away from the road will double your risk of a crash.

FACT: It takes almost a whole minute to type directions on a GPS and get your head refocused on the road! Even using voice commands will take your mind off your driving for about 30 seconds. You get the picture. You can avoid this risk by programming your GPS while you're parked in a safe location (or at home). Need to reprogram it after making a mistake or getting detoured? Pull over before you do that, too.

DON'T READ WHILE DRIVING (EVEN AT STOP SIGNS)

Of course, it's a *terrible* idea for a driver to read something when the car is moving. (That includes everything from test notes to texts to, yes, *directions.*) Surprise: Reading when you're stopped at a light or stop sign is also a hazard. Any time you lose your focus on what's going on around you, you also lose time to react if something goes pear-shaped.

PRACTICE TIP: Find a way to memorize the route ahead of time or to make it feel more familiar. Think of how you learn best at school, then use those skills to memorize your route. For example, maybe you repeat the street names in your head or out loud.

If you learn by watching (or doing), check out Google Street View, which shows you a still photo of the road and its surroundings. (You can move the camera around, "turn" down a street, etc.) This can help you find landmarks like a McDonald's or a red barn, which can help the new route feel more familiar when you drive it.

EXPECT SOME UNEXPECTED DETOURS

Usually, GPS apps connect to a satellite in real time, and they will automatically reroute you if there's an accident or road construction. GPS does this so smoothly (usually) that you might not even realize it. Other times, like if you're driving a familiar route without GPS, you won't know there's a detour until you see the orange signs.

Detours due to road work are planned, so they're often well marked. If not, you can probably follow the stream of cars in front of you. Just keep an eye on signs, too, because other drivers may not follow the detour exactly. If there's an accident or flash flood or something like that, someone in a fluorescent vest will hopefully be pointing out where to go. If you're nervous, you can tell them your destination and ask how to get back on track the fastest.

When a detour is caused by an accident, there probably won't be signs, but there may be a traffic officer directing you where to go. If you're worried about going where they're pointing, you can usually call them over to ask if that's the best route for you. (They're usually local and know the roads well.) Another option is, of course, to find a safe place to pull over, then use a map (paper or digital) to make a new plan.

PRACTICE TIP: The best way to prepare yourself for detours? Keep your gas tank above one-quarter full. That way, you won't have to worry if your journey becomes a few miles longer (or if you wind up stuck in a traffic jam).

Q&A: Ask Someone Else

☐ Can you help me get a local map and find our home on it?

☐ Can you help me figure out our state laws on using GPS?

☐ Can you drive me to a few places while I practice following along on a GPS device, map, or written-out directions?

BEFORE YOU LEAVE

○ **Enter the address** of the destination. (Never do this while driving.)

○ **Double-check the route and destination.** There are 12 cities named Philadelphia in America! It would be awful to be halfway to the wrong one before you realize it.

IN THE CAR

○ **Mount the map screen where you can see it.** If you're not using a built-in system, buy a phone mount or docking station that you can install close to eye level (following your state's laws, of course).

○ **Don't mute the volume between turns.** Some people turn down the GPS volume to listen to music or talk until it's time for next turn. Don't do that. You could miss a turn and you need your hands on the wheel, not the volume selector.

○ **Pull over if you need to reprogram the GPS.** Want to look for a rest stop or restaurant? Need to reroute due to a detour or wrong turn? Find a safe spot in a public parking lot to fix it.

➤ CHAPTER 12:
In the Suburbs: Avoiding Kids, Recycle Bins, and More

Most teens feel pretty chill about driving in the suburbs. More than half of Americans live in suburbia, and driving close to home feels more comfortable. That familiarity and comfort are a problem, because they can make you lower your guard. If your neighborhood has a lot of people your age, you'll also be sharing the roads with a bunch of other new drivers—and they're probably going to be driving at some of the same times that you'll be driving (like before and after school).

Also, although "residential" roads (ones that go through neighborhoods) *look* pretty quiet and low-key, they actually have a lot of hidden hazards. Here's how to spot them.

EXPAND YOUR "SCAN" BEYOND THE ROADWAY

Neighborhoods are full of activity—and *kids*—so you need to be scanning the road with as much focus as you'd have on a highway. Don't limit your gaze to the street and intersections: Expand your "sweep" to include driveways, sidewalks, and front yards, too. The sooner you see something run or roll into the street, the more time you'll have to react.

You could also use your horn to get kids' attention if they're oblivious to you. Just be careful when you use it: You don't want to scare a kid into falling off his bike!

KNOW THE "RIGHT OF WAY" FOR DRIVEWAYS

Surprisingly often, people (including long-time drivers) back out of their driveway without looking—probably thinking "This street's *always* empty." In addition to watching for this when you scan, you should have some idea of what to do when it happens. For example, you can tap your horn to get their attention. (Lightly, if it's not urgent. No need to "yell.") Or, if there's no one behind you, stopping and letting them go first is an option. (We've said it before: Being "right" won't prevent dents and dings.)

Also, don't be "that guy" when *you're* the one entering or exiting a driveway. Look around constantly, using your mirrors and turning your head, to make sure it's clear to exit. Remember that the right of way belongs to anyone already on the roadway or the sidewalk nearby. That includes drivers, pedestrians, and cyclists.

If all this stresses you out, you may want to do a "K turn" so you can exit the driveway in Drive, not Reverse. Of course, you'll need to watch out for people in the *driveway* while doing that maneuver.

---- ----

Stats & Facts

STAT: Kids are twice as likely to be hit by a car between 4 p.m. and 10 p.m. on Halloween than during the same timeframe on any other day of the year.

FACT: It's safest for new drivers to stay off the road during trick-or-treat nights. On those nights, have an adult drive you where you need to go—or just stay home and hand out candy!

"SLOW YOUR ROLL" SO YOU HAVE TIME TO REACT

In many residential areas, the speed limit is 25 miles per hour, even if there's not a sign in sight. Be aware that some of those roads can be really long and straight and have a line down the center, so they may seem like the speed limit would be higher. That's often where police set up speed traps.

School zones, which sometimes are in the middle of a neighborhood, have an even lower speed limit—usually 15 miles per hour at certain times of day.

In addition to easing up on the gas, make sure you keep a safe distance between you and other vehicles. Usually, that's at least 2 seconds behind them. (Count "1 one-thousand, 2 one-thousand"; see Chapter 6.) For bigger vehicles—garbage trucks, delivery trucks, and rental trucks (like moving vans)—leave enough space that you're sure they can see you, too.

---- ----

Stats & Facts

STAT: Intersections are one of the top four reasons that new teen drivers crash.

FACT: Intersections can be places you wouldn't think of, like where a driveway meets a road and where you enter a highway. Basically, wherever you see two roads meet up, you need to be even more on your game than usual.

LOOK OUT FOR ANYTHING THAT COULD BLOCK YOUR VIEW

Parked cars, garbage and recycle bins, freestanding mailboxes, light poles, overgrown shrubs, and fences—these are just a few neighborhood items that can make it tough to see what's ahead or around the corner.

Keep this in mind when you're watching for hazards as well as looking for street signs (if you're following directions) and traffic signs. It's way too easy to blow through stop signs if you're not paying extra attention. This is another reason to be extra cautious and take it slow, especially around intersections and driveways.

DON'T GET CONFUSED BY A FUNERAL

As a passenger, you've probably seen a funeral procession, where a row of cars follows a hearse from the funeral home to the cemetery. As a driver, you'll want to know where that row of cars *ends* and what you should do when you come across a funeral procession.

Generally, all the vehicles in the funeral group must have their headlights and/or flashers on. Sometimes, one or more of the cars will also have a flag or sign that actually says "FUNERAL." Often, the flags are at least on the first and last car, so other drivers can tell who's in the group.

Here's the big yikes, though: Most states have laws that gives cars in a funeral procession the right of way. The first car in line usually has to stop at all stop signs and red lights, but when they start to go, everyone else in line can follow them, even if the light turns red again halfway through.

If you see this kind of thing happening, just sit tight: Don't insert your car into the line or break it up by driving through it, even if it would normally be your turn. But double-check the laws in your state, too, starting with the driver's manual you studied for your driving test.

➤ CHAPTER 13:

Highway Highlights: Managing Merges, Lane Changes, and More

When you're learning a new series of martial arts or dance moves, you can't do all of them really fast on your first try. Often you have to break the whole sequence down into little parts and perfect each part—slowly—before you move on. With highway driving, though, you don't *get* to start out slow. If the speed limit is 65 miles per hour, you can't drag along at 45 just because you're nervous.

If you have your license, that means you've done some highway driving, but if you don't feel super-confident, don't go it alone yet. Ask an adult to help you pick a time when there's not much traffic so you can practice entering and exiting, merging, changing lanes, and passing other vehicles on a highway (even if those vehicles are just make-believe).

While you're getting "up to speed," also look over the following tips, which will help things go more smoothly when you hit the highway on your own someday.

STAY ON TOP OF TOLLS

Sometimes you'll have to pay extra to use a highway or go over a bridge. There used to always be toll booths with people or coin baskets collecting the money, but these are being replaced by electronic collection services.

Many states now have electronic toll-collection systems that you just drive through without stopping. You buy a little device that goes on your windshield, and when you drive through a toll booth, your credit card gets charged automatically. (A few names are E-ZPass, SunPass, Best Pass, and Peach Pass.)

Another no-stop option is "Toll by Plate," where a camera snaps a pic of your license plate and you get a bill in the mail. There will be signs at highway entrances telling you which one is being used.

PRO TIP: When planning your route on a map app, you can request to avoid toll roads. Or you can use a toll calculator website or app to figure out what it will cost you and how you have to pay. If you're going to use a toll road often, getting an electronic pass can save you money: They often charge users a discounted fare.

PLAN FOR PIT STOPS

While you're planning a trip on your favorite map app, look at how far apart the exits are, especially if you're going to be on a particular highway for more than 20 minutes or so. There are some stretches of highway with lots of miles between exits. That means lots of time between bathroom breaks. Most map apps show you where restaurants, rest stops, gas stations, hotels, hospitals, and other important locations are along your route, so you can plan where you'll stop.

PRO TIP: Didn't plan your breaks? Remember that the blue-and-white signs on highways will show you what's available at the next exit. Sometimes a sign will tell you the exact names of the businesses, and other times it'll just give categories, like FOOD, CAMPING, and GAS.

MANAGE YOUR MERGES

Here's the dream: You're on an entrance ramp with a nice, long acceleration lane where you can get up to speed and easily spy a place to merge. The reality? If the entrance ramp isn't long enough for you to do all of that (or if there's a stop sign at the end of it), you'll need to move more quickly once you see an opening. Make sure you can see that nothing is in your lane or the next lane over. It can be tough to tell which lane something is in when it's far away—and other drivers can change lanes at the last second. You want to be *completely* sure it's safe to go. (It'll take you a while to get good at judging the timing, so give yourself more space than you think you'll need.)

Sometimes entrance ramps on really busy highways have a traffic signal at the end of the ramp. This helps space out the flow of cars onto the highway. If the signal is red, you stop, of course. When it turns green, though, that means you *can* go, not that you *should*. Make sure it's safe before you merge.

PRO TIP: You never want to get onto a highway and make the driver behind hit the brakes. That means you need to get up to the speed limit quickly once the coast is clear and you decide to go. Of course, if traffic is going *slower* than the speed limit because it's rush hour or there's an accident, just get up to the speed of the cars around you. Because this is such a tough skill to build, it's a good one to practice with an adult in the car—even after you pass your road test. Asking for extra help with things like this will be proof to your parents that you're taking safety very seriously.

Myths & Truths

MYTH: Drivers won't get a ticket if they're going with the flow of traffic.

TRUTH: If you're going above the speed limit, you can get stopped and ticketed for driving too fast, even if everyone else is, too. You can also get pulled over for driving too slowly, though. That can also be a hazard, especially if you're poking along in the left lane.

Another problem to watch for on highways is unexpected slowdowns or stopped traffic, which can happen due to an accident, road work, or rush hour. To make sure you don't get rear-ended when you have to slow down or stop on a "fast" road, use your rearview mirror to check if the driver behind you is slowing down, too. If not, tap on your brakes three or four times to get their attention, or turn on your flashers. If they're still not stopping, lean on the horn!

- -

STAY IN YOUR LANE (MOSTLY)

As a new driver (who is ideally sticking to the speed limit), you'll probably do best hanging out in the right lane most of the time. In fact, in many states, there's a law that says drivers should drive in the left lane *only* if they're passing another vehicle. Of course, there will be times when road signs tell you to merge left or let you know that your lane is ending or closed. You can't drive when there's no lane, so of course it's OK to get over in those cases. When you do change lanes, always use your turn signal and check all around you to make sure no other driver is about to change lanes, too!

PRO TIP: You should also know when you *must* change lanes. For example, many states have a law that says if you see stopped emergency vehicles with flashing lights (including tow trucks), you must slow down and (only if it's safe to do so) move out of the lane that's closest to the problem. (You can find your state's Move Over Law at drivinglaws.aaa.com/move-over-law/.)

STEER CLEAR OF ROAD RAGE

If you're angry or upset, you shouldn't be driving. In fact, you probably promised that in your driving contract. This means staying chill when other drivers do something you think is dangerous, stupid, or just plain wrong. Try to assume they didn't mean to. (After all, as a new driver, you probably have done some things that fall into those categories.) Even if they *did* do it on purpose, just ignore them and refocus on your own driving. You don't need this distraction!

Also keep in mind that you might do something "wrong" without realizing it—or you might realize it when it's too late to fix it. For instance, maybe you took your turn too soon at an intersection, pulled out in front of someone too slowly on a highway, or drove too slowly in front of them (even if you were doing the speed limit). People have all kinds of stress, and your move may be the last straw for them.

PRO TIP: If you're scared and have a hands-free device, you can call 911 for help. You can keep driving if you're not too shaken up to be safe. If you feel like you need to stop, don't go home. Head for a police station, busy store, or another public location with a lot of people around to help you.

To avoid it getting to that point, the two best things you can do when road rage happens is 1) get away from the other vehicle and 2) don't look at, speak to, or gesture at the other driver. Usually, the enraged person is just a speed demon, and if you let them pass you, they'll be out of your life in seconds. Then you can take a deep breath and get back to enjoying the drive.

NOTE: Keep in mind that the basic tips in Chapter 6 on blind spots, speed limits, and maintaining a safe following distance all apply to highways, too. Also check out the specifics on sharing the road with trucks in Chapter 20.

➤ CHAPTER 14:

Cruising in the Country: Curves, Critters, and More

Adults say taking a drive in the country is *relaxing*. But in fact, you'll need to be *constantly* watching for hazards like wild animals, fallen trees, and one-lane bridges, which you don't see very often if you're more of a city child. To make back-road routes more fun, think of them as a part of a new Mario Kart course—just don't expect any recovery boosts.

No joke, though: It's awful to break down in the middle of nowhere, so before you head for a rural area, make sure your car is in good condition. (If your tires are low on air, fill them up—and fill the gas tank, too.) Also, tell someone what route you'll take and when you expect to arrive. Cell signals can be spotty in the country, so if you get stuck, someone may need to come looking for you.

Think of this chapter as a shortcut through the confusion that can come with driving on back roads.

GO SLOW . . . AND THEN GO EVEN SLOWER

Rural roads tend to be windy, like a river or a rollercoaster. Along with crazy curves, they often have deep dips and high hills, which make it impossible to see up ahead. Often, signs will warn you about these hazards—and they'll even tell you how slow to go. Remember, though, that the speed limit is based on ideal conditions. If there is anything else going on (ice, rain, fog, etc.), you'll need to slow down even more. Another good reason to slow down? Many country roads are edged with ditches and may not have guardrails.

Pay attention to what's coming up on the sides of the road. (Watch for hidden entries like driveways and horse paths, too.) This is another reason to make sure not to zone out on a quiet country road.

PRO TIP: When you see a car coming, get over to the right side of the road as far as safely possible. If it's a dirt road, watch for a dust cloud up ahead, which might be visible before the vehicle. Also, even if the vehicle ahead is a slowpoke, never try to pass on a country road if you can't see way ahead or if you're near a railroad crossing or intersection.

LOOK FOR QUICK CHANGES IN SPEED LIMITS

Many rural roads go through rural towns, and those Main Street sections tend to have a lower speed limit than the rest of the road. You might even have to drop your speed by 10 miles per hour! There are usually extra signs that alert you to the upcoming change—but your best bet is to slow down in these areas anyway.

PRO TIP: Don't think that sleepy towns will ignore speeders. Their police are dedicated to making sure drivers follow the law, and they're happy to ticket those who don't.

Stats & Facts

STAT: About half of the deaths from single-vehicle crashes happen in rural areas.

FACT: You should *always* use your seat belt, and never ride in the back of a pickup truck—even in the country!

TRAIN YOUR EYES ON RAILROAD CROSSINGS

On well-traveled roads, when there's a train crossing there are usually bells, flashing lights, and a gate that lowers down to block traffic. In the country, though, railroad crossings may be marked with only a sign. That means you're the one in charge of checking if a train is coming.

PRO TIP: At every railroad crossing, slow down as you look and listen for a train. You may want to put your window down so you can hear better. Don't cross the tracks unless you are sure nothing is coming. Also be aware that old train tracks may have been turned into walking paths, so watch for hikers and cyclists in these areas, too.

USE YOUR MANNERS AT SINGLE-LANE BRIDGES

Because country roads were created to fit a horse and buggy, they can be very narrow. Over the years, townships have widened many roads, underpasses, and bridges to fit modern two-way traffic, but some one-lane areas still exist—either because they're not used much or because they're historical landmarks (like covered bridges).

PRO TIP: Most of the time, cars on either end of a one-way bridge will take turns crossing. Be prepared for a second driver (or third!) to sneak through, though—and go only when the coast is clear.

Be understanding if another driver takes "your" turn: Often *both* ends of the bridge will say "yield to oncoming traffic," which makes it confusing. If you both followed the rule, you'd never go anywhere.

GET USED TO USING YOUR HIGH BEAMS

If most of your driving is in well-lit areas, you may never have used your high beams before. In the country, though, there's often no artificial light around. If the moon isn't bright, it can be really, really hard to see. If you click on your high beams, you'll be able to see farther ahead, but be ready to switch them off quickly if another car is coming. Dawn, dusk, and nighttime are all good times to put on these lights and to slow down a bit.

The rest of the day, it doesn't hurt to leave your headlights on, as long as you remember to turn them off when you park. They can help drivers see you sooner in dark, wooded areas, and you won't need to fumble for the switch when entering a tunnel.

PRO TIP: Practice using your high beams on an empty road or driveway near home, so you can be quick about turning them on and off.

Myths & Truths

MYTH: If your car starts to skid, you should hit the brakes.

TRUTH: Experts actually advise that you NOT do this. Instead, gently turn your steering wheel in the same direction as you're sliding. You'll probably overcorrect a little bit and wind up skidding the other way. But usually the second skid is smaller. Just turn into it, too. Repeat this process until you're back in control. It usually won't take very long.

KNOW THE DANGERS OF DIRT AND DEBRIS

Dirt, gravel, and potholes all can cause your tires to lose their grip, which can cause you to slide sideways. A cloud of dust kicked up by tires can block your view. Rain can turn a dirt road into mud. Kicked-up gravel can crack your windshield. Driving over a big stone or pothole can make your wheels lose traction, and it can damage the underside of your car. And there's a good reason that people use the phrase "getting stuck in a rut." Sometimes it happens for real. And ruts are often in the middle of the road, which can make it tough to maneuver out of the way if something's coming.

PRO TIPS: If the road isn't in great condition, slow down—but do it carefully. Slamming on the brakes and cutting the wheel can both cause skidding. A few more nonskid tips:

- Leave more space than usual if the car ahead is kicking up dust or gravel.

- When going down a steep hill on an unpaved road, shift into a low gear rather than over-using your brakes.

- Don't try to cross flowing water or drive into a patch of water if you're not sure how deep it is.

KEEP CALM IF CRITTERS ARE CROSSING

When animals are crossing the road, keep in mind that they're not in your way—*you're* cutting through *their* living room. In the country, you might see livestock wandering across the road during the day, or you might come across deer, foxes, raccoons, possums, cats, and other wildlife. Passing a farm? Don't be surprised if a dog runs alongside your car.

You'll need to scan constantly, watching the road and the surrounding areas, watching for movement. If you see an animal, slow down and honk your horn to scare them away. If they dart into the road, don't swerve! We know it seems mean, but animals have pretty good instincts, and they'll usually get themselves out of the way if you're not speeding. If not, you'll be safer if you hit an animal than if you lose control and hit a tree or wind up in a ditch.

PRO TIP: Animals often travel in groups. If you see *one* cross, expect there to be others nearby. Wait until they have all crossed over and are a safe distance away. (This includes cows, sheep, and other farm animals.) Never try to drive "through" a herd. That can make them more likely to run into your car. Also watch for two-footed animals—walking, cycling, riding an ATV, etc. They live in the country, too!

CHECK IT OUT: RURAL REASONS TO SLOW WAAAAY DOWN

When driving in the country, watch for these rural
hazards and slow down when you see them:

- ○ An approaching vehicle (if there's no shoulder or the road is narrow)
- ○ Fallen branches or something else in the road
- ○ Farm equipment, a horse and buggy, or another slow-moving vehicle
- ○ A town, neighborhood, or hidden driveway
- ○ Heavy darkness (in a wooded area or at night, dusk, etc.)
- ○ A one-lane bridge or underpass
- ○ A tunnel through a mountain
- ○ An ungated railroad crossing
- ○ Bad weather (including something as simple as a storm, which can knock down tree branches)
- ○ Bad road conditions (potholes, mud, dust clouds, etc.)
- ○ An animal-crossing sign or actual animals (in or beside the road)

➤ CHAPTER 15:
City Life: One-Way Streets, Double-Parked Cars, and More

Cities are busiest in the morning . . . and at lunchtime . . . and, well, basically all day, every weekday. It may get a *little* quieter when city workers are home for the evening, but that's when the nightlife starts.

The least amount of city traffic is usually very early on a weekend, so that's the best time to practice city driving. If you've never driven in a city before (or haven't done it much), it's not a good thing to do solo. (Luckily, cities offer plenty of other ways to get around!)

Before your first drive into a city, ask an adult to take you in as a passenger. Practice looking around for hazards and notice how little time there is to react. Ask if your driver will point out what they're seeing and what they're doing, too. ("I see a delivery van ahead, so I'm hovering my foot over the brake in case I have to stop.")

For safety's sake (and your sanity), fill your tank before you go, and keep your doors locked and windows up the whole time you're there. (Locked doors are a good idea anywhere, really.) Also keep in mind these expert tips:

REVIEW THE ROUTE AHEAD OF TIME

Driving in the city is confusing! Even though a city's streets may form a grid (like graph paper), there's always the random diagonal street or city park that breaks the pattern. Broadway and Central Park in New York City are two examples. Reading street signs can be a challenge, too, since there is so much going on around you. If you're in a state that doesn't allow you to use GPS, this can all be very tough without someone in the passenger seat to help you navigate.

PRO TIP: Use your favorite map app to look at the city—or find one on the city's tourism website. You can also search the city's name and "map with landmarks." Attractions like statues, shops, and parks are easier to spot than street signs!

KEEP YOUR EYES ON THE BLOCK AHEAD

When you're scanning a highway with your eyes, you're looking at about a quarter mile of roadway. In the city, that's about the size of a city block.

PRO TIP: Try not to end up stuck in traffic behind a big vehicle like a truck or delivery van. It can block your view of signs (and hazards), and you might miss a turn.

Stats & Facts

STAT: On a three-lane road, the center lane is usually the least crowded.

FACT: That's because many people in the left and right lanes are getting ready to turn or are slowed down by vehicles parking or making frequent stops. Try to keep to the center lane when driving in the city, but don't wait until the last second to change lanes when it's time to turn.

HOVER YOUR FOOT OVER THE BRAKE

This is known as "covering the brake," and it's something you should do whenever you see a potential problem ahead—in the city, the country, or wherever. In the city, though, it's even *more* important because the cars are so close together, so you have very little time to stop. Having your foot already in place (instead of on the gas) gives you a split second more time to react.

Covering the brake is different from *riding* the brake. Riding the brake means resting your foot ON the brake, which turns on your brake lights. That's not good for the brakes. Also, having brake lights flash on is something other drivers watch for, so they get ready to stop, too. If you're riding the brake all the time, that warning "flash" never happens.

PRO TIP: Cover the brake when you see a crosswalk sign start flashing. When that happens, it means the sign is about to change . . . and the traffic signal will change shortly after it.

LOOK TWICE FOR ONE-WAY STREET SIGNS

If you miss a turn, you can often just take the next turn instead . . . but not always. Sometimes the next street will be going one way the *wrong* way. One-way streets will be well marked, but you have to *look* for the signs. Never assume a city street goes both directions!

Also watch out for areas where a one-way street becomes a two-way street (usually at an intersection). Again, it's marked, but if you don't see the signs, you might think the other drivers are heading the wrong way!

PRO TIP: When you're turning onto a one-way street, look *both* ways. There could be pedestrians or cyclists coming from the other direction—or a driver who made a wrong turn.

Myths & Truths

MYTH: Roundabouts and traffic circles are dangerous.

TRUTH: Research has shown that there are fewer crashes at traffic circles than at traditional crisscross intersections because drivers have to slow down to merge into them. In fact, traffic circles can lower the risk of accidents that cause injury or loss of life by about 80%.

LEARN THE INS AND OUTS OF ROUNDABOUTS

Circular intersections are popping up in more suburban areas these days, but they're still most common in or near cities. When entering a roundabout, you'll be going in a counterclockwise direction around a center island (sometimes with a statue in the middle). To join the circle, you need to sort of merge left like you do when entering a highway's right lane.

The first time you use a traffic circle it may feel weird, but they're actually safer than other types of intersections, which is why they're used. They force drivers to slow down, and because everyone's going in the *same* direction (unlike a four-way intersection), it's easier to pull out safely.

PRO TIP: As with other intersections, you need to yield to the traffic that's already in the roundabout and enter only when it's clear. There may be a traffic light or flashing lights to help pace things out.

LOOK FOR LANE-CONTROL SIGNALS AT BRIDGES AND TUNNELS

City bridges, tunnels, and entry points often have lots of lanes in a row. That doesn't mean you can use any one you want to. Above the lanes there is usually a signal that lights up with one of three things: a green arrow (pointing down), a yellow X, or a red X.

The green arrow means that lane is open, the yellow X means you should start to merge into a green-arrow lane when it's safe, and the red X means you shouldn't be in that lane at all. (Toll areas also have these signals sometimes.)

PRO TIP: Also watch for "turn arrow" signs in left and right lanes. If you're in a lane with a sign that shows an arrow curving to the left, you have to make a left turn (unless you can safely merge into a different lane).

CHECK IT OUT: HIDDEN HAZARDS OF THE CITY

When you're scanning the road for hazards, you need to know what you're looking for. Here are a few of the potential problems for drivers in the city:

○ **Parking:** Watch for cars that are trying to parallel park, that are double-parked (stopped in traffic with no driver inside), or that are stopped and have people getting in or out.

○ **Deliveries:** Delivery trucks make a lot of stops, with the driver running in and out of buildings nearby. Also watch for delivery *bicycles*, which like to zip in and out of traffic.

○ **Paid transportation:** City buses and tour buses stop often. Taxis and ride-sharing vehicles also can stop unexpectedly.

○ **Alleys:** Cyclists like to zoom through alleys as a shortcut. Wider alleys may have other types of vehicles coming in or out, too. Whenever you see a break in the line of buildings, be prepared for something to pop out.

○ **Illegal crossings:** Many pedestrians and cyclists don't follow the rules when crossing city streets. Tourists may not even know what the rules are. Keep an eye out for people on foot *everywhere*, not just at intersections or crosswalks.

○ **Traffic lights:** Just because the light turns green, that doesn't mean it's safe to go. Very often, drivers or pedestrians will try to beat the light, so look both ways before you take your foot off the brake.

➤ CHAPTER 16:

Driving to School: Bus Safety, School Parking, and More

You *love* driving to school. No. More. School. Bus. Ever.

Problem: Now you have to learn what to do when you're *behind* one of those things. How far away do you have to stop? What about at an intersection? On a highway?

We got you. Here's what to watch out for, plus a few notes on dealing with the school parking lot.

EXPECT SCHOOL BUSES TO ACT STRANGELY

By law, bus drivers have to do some things other drivers don't. For example, they may have to drive slower than the posted speed limit. At all railroad crossings, they have to stop, open their door, and look and listen for a train— even if there are gates and signals. (Trucks with dangerous chemicals do this, too.) And even if it's usually legal to turn "right on red," school buses might have to wait for green. Even if you don't know the exact laws, just know that this stuff might happen. It's one reason you should keep about 3 car lengths behind a bus whenever possible. Driving schools also recommend yielding the right of way to school buses at all times, even if it's not always the law.

EXPECT STUDENTS TO ACT STRANGELY, TOO

Kids are hyper. They drop things, run into the street, shove their friends, and generally don't pay attention. (We know you remember.) They might be standing in the street—like if there's a huge puddle or pile of snow at the bus stop. Now you know why parents look so stressed all the time.

Whenever you're driving near a group of kids (or even just a few), it's a good idea to slow down and "cover" the brake (hover over it with your foot). See Chapter 15 for more on this tactic and when else to do it.

Stats & Facts

STAT: Fines for failing to stop for a school bus with red flashers can be as much as $1,000.

FACT: Some states will *also* suspend your driver's license for a month or more. Some even allow for JAIL time! Many buses are now equipped with cameras, too, so it's easier than ever to get caught in the act. Of course, the best reason to stop is to protect the kids around you.

STAY OUT OF THE DANGER ZONE

The 10-foot area all the way around the bus is called the "danger zone" for a good reason. This is where kids are most at risk of getting hit. The danger zone also includes the areas where kids walk to get to and from the bus.

You should never pass a stopped school bus with flashing lights because it's unsafe—which is why it's also illegal. In fact, two-thirds of kids who die near a school bus are hit by someone trying to pass the bus.

If you and the bus are both moving (and it's otherwise legal and safe to pass), remember that the bus driver has huge blind spots (just like tractor-trailer drivers do). So don't hang out alongside the bus for any longer than you need to.

DOUBLE-CHECK YOUR STATE'S "STOPPING" LAWS

You should ALWAYS stop when a school bus stops to pick up or drop off kids. The one exception is a bus stopping on a highway, and even then, it depends on the specific conditions of the stop. You don't need to stop if:

- You're driving on a highway AND

- You're going the opposite direction of the bus AND

- There is a *physical barrier* between you and the bus.

Physical barriers are things like guard rails, concrete barriers, a row of trees or shrubs, a stream, or a grass "median." One of the things that differs from state to state is whether you can keep going if it's 2 lanes, 3 lanes, or 4 lanes.

Most states' Department of Transportation website will have illustrations or videos that can help you see what's allowed (and not).

STAY ULTRA-FOCUSED WHEN YOU'RE IN THE (SCHOOL) ZONE

The areas around schools are marked as "school zones" to protect students going to and from school on foot, bike, scooter, or whatever. These areas usually are well marked with flashing lights, speed limit signs, and speed bumps. There may also be crossing guards and/or police officers directing traffic. Obviously, do what they tell you to.

During certain hours—usually 7 a.m. to 9 a.m. and 2 p.m. to 4 p.m.—you'll need to slow down to the "school zone speed limit," which can be as low as 10 miles per hour. It's really hard to drive that slowly. You may need to keep your foot partway on the brake most of the time, then tap the gas lightly to keep going.

Keep in mind that you may drive through a few other school zones before you get to *your* school.

Myths & Truths

MYTH: When you reach an intersection with a bus, you don't have to stop unless you have a stop sign.

TRUTH: If the bus is loading or unloading at an intersection, you MUST stop, whether or not you have a stop sign.

Don't try to turn, either, even if you would be headed in the opposite direction. That's illegal, too.

Just stay put until all the things in "Check It Out" show you it's clear to go again. The *easiest* way to know when it's safe to go is to wait until the bus starts moving again. Of course, wait your turn if there are other cars around.

FIND OUT YOUR HIGH SCHOOL'S PARKING RULES

Many high schools make you pay for a parking tag or sticker that you put in a window or hang on your rearview mirror. (If it's a hang-tag, remember to take it down while you're driving so it won't block your view and so you won't get a ticket.)

If you share a few different cars with your family, you'll usually need to register all of them. When you pick up your tag, make sure you know what lot you're allowed to park in, too. (They might tell you "Lot C" but the lots often aren't actually marked!)

If you're staying or returning for after-school activities, you're usually allowed to park closer to the building, but ask about that, too.

SAVE YOURSELF SOME STRESS IN THE PARKING LOT

You already know the school parking lot is a mess at the end of the day. Plus, most teens say they sit in their cars making sure they look good, listening to the end of a song, talking to a friend, or looking at their phone. Those who are walking probably are doing some of these things, too, so you've got to pay attention. Here are a few ways to make it easier on yourself:

- **Do a practice run** with a parent or driving instructor—during the crazy hours, if possible. Have the adult help you find the student lot, practice parking, and point out possible hazards.

- **Go to school a little early** and leave a little late so you'll miss the rush. It may take you a few tries to figure out the best timing. (Depending on your teachers, you might be able to get out of your last class a little early if you need to be somewhere right after school.)

- **Park at the farthest end of the student lot,** where there will be more spaces, fewer cars, and fewer people walking.

- **Stay focused:** This means no phone—even when you're walking from the lot to the building.

- **If possible, park so that you can pull forward to exit,** instead of backing up.

- **Pick the easiest exit,** even if it's not the closest or the best one for where you're going.

- **Go really slowly and wear your seat belt at all times**—even if you're just driving from the student lot to a spot near the band room or the gym.

- -

Stats & Facts

STAT: You need to stop 10 to 30 feet from a school bus with red flashing lights. (The specific distance varies by state.)

FACT: Here are some numbers to help you estimate how far away you are:

☐ A compact sedan is about 15 feet long

☐ A regular-size school bus is about 45 feet long

If you're not driving in your home state, you probably won't know the legal distance, so leave a few car lengths, to be safe.

- - - - - - - - - - - - - - - - - - [?] - - - - - - - - - - - - - - - - - -

Q&A: Ask Yourself

☐ Do I know my state law on stopping behind a school bus with red flashing lights?

☐ Do I know the rules for parking at school?

☐ Should I try to find a route to school with fewer buses and bus stops?

- -

CHECK IT OUT: WHEN TO STOP NEAR A SCHOOL BUS

Like just about every other type of road rules, school bus rules vary by state. So, look up the specifics in your driver's manual and write down the differences here. Generally speaking:

WHEN BEHIND A SCHOOL BUS:

O Scan for kids standing around or walking.

O Stay at least 3 car lengths behind the bus so they see you and so you'll have time to stop when they do.

O Don't drive alongside a bus for more than a few seconds because much of that area is in the driver's blind spot.

WHEN AMBER LIGHTS ARE FLASHING:

O This means that the bus will stop within a few hundred feet.

O Slow down and watch for kids.

O If you're right behind the bus, back off so you'll have enough room to stop.

O If you're driving toward the bus (on the opposite side of the street), slow down if you won't be past the bus by the time it stops.

O If you're already alongside the bus, continue on, while watching for kids.

O If you're in front of the bus (and going the same direction), keep driving.

O If you're at an intersection, stop and stay stopped.

WHEN RED LIGHTS ARE FLASHING:

O Never pass a school bus with red lights flashing.

O Stop several car lengths away from the bus. (The law varies by state, but it's never less than 10 feet.)

- Be *completely* stopped when the stop sign and/ or stop signal arm are extended.
- Remain stopped while kids get on or off.
- Keep your foot on the brake while you wait.

YOU MAY START DRIVING AGAIN WHEN:

- The red flashing lights are turned off AND
- The stop sign and/or stop signal arm is withdrawn AND
- All the children are safely away from the road.
- Some states also require you to remain stopped until the bus begins to move again.

➤ CHAPTER 17:
Driving for Work: Laws, Exemptions, and More

With all your new driving expenses, you'll probably be looking for a job (if you don't have one already). When you decide to apply, consider whether you are OK with driving FOR work or if you would rather just drive TO and FROM work. (*None of the above* is also an option, if your workplace is farther from home than you're ready to go.) This can help you decide between taking a job in pizza delivery versus at a supermarket checkout.

Here are some things you should know before taking on driving as a work responsibility.

THINK ABOUT THE TIMES YOU'LL BE DRIVING

Driving instructors agree: You shouldn't rush into rush-hour driving. The hazards are multiplied because there are more drivers, and those drivers are more likely to be stressed and, as a result, more than a little bit touchy. That's a recipe for road rage.

Nighttime driving is *also* more challenging for new drivers. Not only will you find it harder to see what's on the road, but also you might be tired from a full day of school, after-school activities, and whatever else you cram into a day.

If you can't avoid driving at these times, ask an adult to do a test run with you. This way you'll get to practice the route with another set of (trained) eyes on traffic.

FIND OUT IF YOU NEED EXTRA PAPERWORK

Many states have Graduated Driver Licensing laws that restrict young drivers from being on the road at certain times of day. However, you can usually get an exemption for driving that's related to your job, after-school activities, or religious or volunteer events.

Check with your state's Department of Transportation to find out what official papers you'll need to carry with you when driving during "off" hours. (You may need to show it to a police officer if you get stopped.)

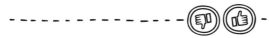

Myths & Truths

MYTH: After age 18, you can drive anywhere for an employer.

TRUTH: You're not allowed to drive a commercial vehicle across state lines until you turn 21.

GET TRAINED ON ANY NEW-TO-YOU VEHICLES

If you're going to be driving a vehicle owned by your employer, you'll need to learn about its safety features and the basics (like how to use the windshield wipers). Government agencies suggest that employers provide driver training to young workers, but if yours doesn't, ask your boss to give you the rundown.

Make sure you feel completely comfortable with driving the vehicle before you go out alone. Don't be afraid to admit it if you're not: Your boss would rather get the truth than have to fill out paperwork about a fender bender.

KNOW THAT EMPLOYERS MAY HAVE STRICTER RULES

You'll find a summary of the laws on young drivers in "Check It Out." Some employers take it a step further and restrict young workers even more. For example, they may let young drivers go on only one driving run per workday instead of the two they're allowed.

Stats & Facts

STAT: At age 17, teens can drive for only 20% of their workweek.

FACT: We did the math for you: For a 10-hour workweek, that's 2 hours. For a 15-hour workweek, it's 3 hours. For a 20-hour workweek, it's 4 hours.

TALK WITH YOUR BOSS ABOUT CELL PHONE USAGE

When you're driving, you need to focus. You may feel safer if you put your work phone to sleep when you drive. If you're going to do that, let your boss know ahead of time, so they don't worry or wonder where you are. In some states, it's illegal for young drivers to use these devices even in hands-free mode. Also, if you have to text or talk with your boss while you're out, don't do it while driving, no matter what. Find a safe place to pull over, then reach out.

EXPECT THEM TO CHECK ON YOUR DRIVING

Your boss may recheck your driving record after you're hired to make sure you haven't gotten a ticket or been in an accident. If either of these things have happened, it's best if you're the one to tell your boss, rather than having them find out on their own. Employers may also do ride-alongs so they can see how well you're driving—and offer ways to improve.

If your boss cuts back your driving time, don't take it personally. They might be trying to spread the work around evenly, or they might be trying to keep you safe.

Finally, don't be afraid to tell your boss if you want to *stop* driving for work, even if you've been doing it for a while. To be safe behind the wheel, you need to feel comfortable and confident there.

CHECK IT OUT: DRIVING LAWS FOR 17-YEAR-OLD WORKERS

The U.S. Department of Labor Wage and Hour Division has created laws specifically about teens driving as part of their job. Drivers aged 16 and younger are not allowed to drive for work at all, unless it's a farm-related job. Adults aged 18 and older have lots more freedom to drive for work. (Check the website youthrules.gov for tons of info on this.) It's the 17-year-olds who have lots of rules to follow.

In addition to the requirements listed here, you will *also* need to follow your state's laws and only do what your level of driver's license allows you to, whether it's a learner's permit, junior license, or unrestricted license.

BEFORE DRIVING AT WORK, 17-YEAR-OLDS MUST:

- O Have a valid state driver's license
- O Have completed a state-approved driver's ed course
- O Have NO moving violations (like speeding tickets) when hired

WHEN DRIVING FOR WORK, 17-YEAR-OLDS CAN ONLY DRIVE:

- O During daylight hours
- O Within 30 miles of the workplace
- O For a maximum 2 trips per workday
- O For only 33% of their work shift
- O For only 20% of their weekly hours
- O In a car or truck that weighs 6,000 pounds or less
- O In a vehicle with seat belts for everyone in it

SOME OF THE THINGS 17-YEAR-OLDS CANNOT DO:

- O Make time-sensitive deliveries (like pizza!)
- O Have more than 3 passengers, including coworkers
- O Have a job where driving is the *main* duty (like a valet or shuttle driver)
- O Tow other vehicles

SECTION 4:

STEERING CLEAR OF TROUBLE: BE READY FOR ANYTHING

Some new drivers worry about what "might" happen. That's less of a problem if you have a Plan A in place to avoid pitfalls . . . and a Plan B for dealing with them if they do happen. Lucky for you, that's what this part of the book is all about.

➤ CHAPTER 18:
How to Weather
Any Weather

If you're not in the habit of checking the weather every morning, this is a good time to start. Now that you're driving, the weather will affect more than what you wear and whether your after-school practice gets canceled. By knowing what's coming, you can avoid driving in conditions you're not ready for—or ask an adult to ride along and guide you.

Many weather-related issues cause similar problems, including low visibility, slippery roads, flooding, and fallen wires or trees. Here are some ways to sidestep these issues—and to deal with them if you get caught off guard.

WHEN THE WEATHER IS BLOCKING YOUR VIEW

Rain, snow, smog, fog, dust, and smoke (from wildfires, for example) all make it hard to see street markings, stop signs, signal lights, and everything else on the road. If you're caught in these conditions:

- **Turn on your headlights.** In many states, the law says you must turn on your headlights whenever your windshield wipers are going. Don't use your high beams, since the particles in the air will reflect the light and make it even harder to see. Remember that *other* drivers may forget to put their lights on, so keep a sharp lookout for unlit cars, too.

- **Drive very slowly and leave extra room** between yourself and other vehicles. Now's not the time to do anything tricky like trying to pass.

- If you are coming up to a stop sign or light, **begin to brake as early as possible** and do it very slowly. That gives drivers behind you more of a chance to notice your brake lights.

- If the rain is too fast for your wipers to clear (or you otherwise feel it's unsafe to drive), **find a place to pull over ASAP.** Get as far off the road as safely possible, turn on your emergency flashers, and leave your seat belt on until it's safe to drive.

Myths & Truths

MYTH: When it's snowy or icy, you only have to worry about cleaning off your car windows and windshields.

TRUTH: You need to clear the top of your car (roof and hood) of ice and snow, too. If you don't, a hunk can slide off into another vehicle or pedestrian and cause an accident.

WHEN THE ROAD IS SLIPPERY (OR MIGHT BE)

Did you know that roads are likely to get slick in the first 10 minutes of a rainstorm? The water causes oil and dirt to rise to the street's surface, creating a thin film that can make your car skid or hydroplane. Rain can also turn leaf piles into a slippery mess or turn dirt roads muddy. A few tips to help you avoid sliding around:

- Watch for road signs that say things like "slippery when wet" or "bridge freezes before road surface." These are definitely trouble spots. Bridges and shady areas are also most likely to freeze before other stretches of road.

- Slow down *below* the speed limit and leave more distance between your vehicle and others.

- Avoid driving over black ice—where the road looks wet but is actually icy. This can happen any time the road is wet and the temperature is at or below freezing.

- Whenever you need to brake, try to do it very slowly and gently so you won't skid. If you're coming to an intersection, try to time the light so you don't have to completely stop. Also try to avoid having to stop on a slippery uphill road.

- If you're going downhill, shift into low gear to help slow down the car naturally.

- If you're stopped on a slippery road, accelerate slowly when it's time to go. Going too fast too soon can melt the snow under your tires, turning it into ice.

WHEN THERE'S A RISK OF FLOODING

Flooding can happen when rain falls so fast that the ground can't absorb it, and rain can cause creeks and rivers to rise. Water can also collect in unexpected places, like on a parking lot or a dip in the road. Some tips to avoid getting swept away:

- Don't drive on bridges that have fast-moving water underneath. (They can wash out without warning.)

- Don't drive through flood waters. The mantra here is: "Turn around, don't drown."

- Never drive around barricades, even if you "think" you can make it.

- If you live on a coast or near the bank of a river or lake that often floods, visit ready.gov/floods to learn more about this topic, including how to evacuate.

---- ----

Stats & Facts

STAT: Hydroplaning can happen at just 35 miles per hour in just a tenth of an inch of water.

FACT: Hydroplaning is when your vehicle slides over the surface of the road on top of a thin film of water. The faster you drive, the greater the risk of hydroplaning. It's also more likely if you're driving on tires with worn tread.

If you do hydroplane, keep both hands on the wheel and ease off the gas pedal. (Quick braking or turning will cause a skid.) As you slow down, your tires will regain their grip naturally. This can be really scary, so you may want to talk to your driving instructor for more advice on this topic.

Stats & Facts

STAT: Just 12 inches of flood water can sweep away a vehicle, even a large one.

FACT: Never drive into water if you can't tell how deep it is. And don't try to "rescue" your car if it's parked in an area that's flooding. Just 6 inches of flood water can knock you off your feet.

WHEN POWER LINES OR DEBRIS HAS FALLEN

High winds and heavy ice can cause power lines and tree branches (or whole trees) to fall onto roadways. The common advice here is to call 911 and report it right away (after you've pulled over safely somewhere, of course). Some other tips:

- If you see a fallen power line, never touch it, and avoid driving over it. If a tree fell *on* the power line, don't touch *either* of them!

- If a power line falls on your car with you inside, stay put until emergency workers arrive and tell you what to do. Ask the 911 operator to stay on the line so they can tell you what to do if conditions worsen (like a fire starts).

- If there's debris on the road that's not blocking travel completely, don't brake hard: Slow down gradually and drive slowly around the debris when the coast is clear. Don't put yourself in danger by trying to remove it yourself.

WHEN IT'S SNOWING HARD (OR ABOUT TO)

Driving in winter weather can be unnerving even for adultier adults. In fact, everyone should stay off the roads if possible when a winter storm is brewing (or in progress). That's especially true for new drivers! Here are some ways to stay safer when it's snowy out:

- *Before* the first snowstorm, stock your trunk with blankets and cold-weather gear (boots, gloves/mittens, hat, scarf, coat). Do this *especially* if you don't usually wear these things when driving! (Lots of high school students stick to sneakers and hoodies all year.)

- If your car's parked in snow, clear out around the exhaust pipe before starting the engine. This will prevent carbon monoxide from building up inside your car, which can be deadly in a matter of minutes. (While you shovel out, ask passengers to wait outside of the car so you know they'll be safe.)

- When there's snow on the ground (or falling), turn down your music and put down your window. Snow can muffle the sounds around you, making it harder for you to hear horns, sirens, or other sounds nearby.

- Watch for people in unusual places. When snow blocks the sidewalks, people may wind up where you wouldn't expect them—like walking on the road. Kids might also be out, pulling a sled or having a snowball fight.

WHEN YOU'RE IN A NATURAL-DISASTER AREA

More information on weather hazards can be found on the website of the Department of Homeland Security at Ready.gov. There are also tips on what to do if there's an earthquake, hurricane, tornado, tsunami, volcano eruption, wildfire, or other emergency. If any of these events are possible where you live (or where you drive), it's worth skimming the web pages for their expert advice on how to deal.

CHECK IT OUT: WHAT TO KNOW ABOUT PHONE ALERTS

Driving by yourself means you need to know more about what's going on around you, since there won't be an adult to guide you. Good news: If you have a cell phone that supports it, you *already* are set up to receive FREE text messages called Wireless Emergency Alerts (WEAs).

TYPES OF WIRELESS EMERGENCY ALERTS:

- Extreme weather
- Local emergencies
- Presidential alerts (about a national emergency)
- AMBER Alerts (about missing children)
- Silver Alerts (about missing seniors/older adults)
- Blue Alerts (about violent criminals on the loose)

TYPES OF NATIONAL WEATHER SERVICE ALERTS:

- Extreme alerts (for tsunamis, tornadoes, extreme winds, hurricanes, and typhoons)
- Severe alerts (for storm surges, flash floods, dust storms, and snow squalls)

When an alert comes in, your phone will vibrate and you'll hear a special tone. If this happens, find a safe place to pull over before looking at the message. The WEA text will include what type of alert it is, the hours that it's active, and what you should do next.

➤ CHAPTER 19:

Workarounds for Road Work, Debris, and Potholes

People who live in Toledo, Ohio, claim the four seasons there are Fall, Winter, Spring, and Road Construction. For Bostonians, they're Almost Winter, Winter, Still Winter. . . and Road Construction. You get the picture: Summer equals road work. (Of course, it can happen other times of year, too, but this is when you'll notice it the most.) You might know about road work months in advance: Sometimes crews put up signs to let drivers know the dates of upcoming road work. If not, you can use a map app to precheck your route and see if there are any slowdowns you'd want to avoid.

When you just *can't* avoid these work zones, tap your memory for these tips:

FOLLOWING THE SIGNS PROTECTS YOU, TOO

Before road work begins, its leaders come up with a plan to direct drivers around or through it. These plans—which include signs, signals, barriers, etc.—are designed to protect everyone, including you and your passengers. Many work zone crashes happen because drivers ignore these plans and try to keep driving as usual. Some people are too distracted and don't see the road work signs. Don't be those guys. Follow the plan the best you can.

Myths & Truths

MYTH: Road workers are at greater risk than drivers.

TRUTH: In a recent year, 85% of deaths in work zone crashes were drivers and passengers, not crew members. By following the rules in these areas, you're not just protecting the workers—you're keeping yourself and *your* "crew" safe, too.

WATCH FOR EARLY WARNING SIGNS

If you're scanning the road ahead, you'll easily spot signs of upcoming construction. These can include work-zone speed limit signs, a police car with flashers, people wearing reflective vests and holding flags, digital signs with arrows or messages, and physical barriers like cones, barrels, and concrete barriers. You may even see a "pilot car," which is an official vehicle that drives at the front of the line of traffic to ensure that everyone behind them slows down before they reach the work zone. (Never try to pass the pilot car.)

Don't get *distracted* by all these visuals, but do read any written messages, so you know what to do next. And use them as a cue to sit up straight and really focus on what's up ahead.

USE YOUR LIGHTS TO ALERT OTHER DRIVERS

In some states, it's required by law to turn on headlights when driving through a work zone—day or night. This includes work zones where it doesn't look like anyone is working. Sometimes, road construction is broken into several shifts, including a night shift, so never assume it's completely deserted. It can be annoying when crews leave these signs out long after the work appears to have been completed, but heed them anyway because you never know. Plus you can be fined for failing to follow the rules.

If you're driving slower than the speed limit and there's nothing behind you, put on your four-way flashers to get the attention of approaching drivers. This is especially helpful on highways, where people are *expecting* to keep zooming along at 65 miles per hour. Using your headlights and flashers also shows the road crew that you're paying attention.

UNDERSTAND THE METHODS OF MERGING

Often, road work requires the shutdown of at least one of the lanes of traffic. If so, you may see signs like "left lane ends," which will likely tell you how many feet or miles you are away from the merge and which lane to get into. These usually start a mile or two before the merge point, so you'll have plenty of time. Don't panic and feel like you need to move over right away!

There's a huge debate about whether it's better to merge ASAP after you see these signs or wait until the last minute. The second approach is called a *zipper merge*, because the cars (ideally) take turns heading into the single lane, like teeth on a zipper. For the zipper method to work, each of the drivers in the continuing lane has to let in one car from the lane that's ending. This can be a trigger for road rage because some people view this as "cutting in line."

So, what should *you* do? As a new driver, you're probably better off merging as soon as it's safe, rather than waiting until the last minute. You won't make people mad, and you'll likely have more room to change lanes, which will be less stressful, too. (Don't forget to use your turn signal when merging.)

Of course, when you get to the spot where the roads merge, you should kindly "let in" one of the cars that's using the zipper method. Who says you can't have it both ways?

LEAVE PLENTY OF ROOM AROUND YOU

Traffic might seem super-controlled in a work zone, but that doesn't mean that the driver ahead won't slam on the brakes for some reason. So stay at a safe following distance as you go through the work zone.

Also, know that the work-zone planners have left you plenty of room to make your way through to the other side, even if those concrete barriers make you feel trapped in a tight spot. Big rigs have to make it through, too: If they can fit, so can you. Just imagine you're parking between two cars, keep yourself centered, and remember to breathe.

WATCH OUT FOR ROAD WORKERS GONE ROGUE

Don't count on the road crew to be paying attention to traffic. Even though they get safety training, they're still human and can make mistakes. They can get distracted by what they're doing, trip, get injured, or jog across the road to a portable toilet. Keep an eye on them just like you do kids in a neighborhood. And give them the right of way if you see them trying to cross.

BE CAREFUL WHEN GETTING OUT OF THE ZONE

At the end of the work zone, use your turn signal and get back into the right lane of traffic (if you're not already there). This allows traffic behind you to flow out of the zone more quickly and smoothly. It also puts you in the lane you should be traveling in when you're not passing anyone, which is probably where you want to be. Slowly return to the normal speed limit, while keeping a cushion of space between you and the car ahead. (You can sigh with relief and relax your shoulders, too.)

CHECK IT OUT: HOW TO AVOID STUFF IN THE ROAD

Tens of thousands of crashes each year involve road debris. Basically, that includes anything that's in the road that *shouldn't* be, such as car parts from an accident, tree branches, roadkill, and things that fell off vehicles, like mufflers, tire treads, mattresses, and garbage bags. Sometimes they'll land in the road, and other times they'll strike other cars while airborne. That's another reason not to mess with your playlist while you're driving, even if the song is really bad.

Potholes are another unpleasant surprise that may be lurking in your traffic lane. These can also cause damage to cars, especially if they're deep or you hit them just right (or just wrong). Luckily, the tips for dealing with these issues are basically the same.

DEALING WITH DEBRIS AND POTHOLES

O Always maintain a safe following distance from the car in front of you and scan the road about a half-mile ahead. Watch for anything weird in the roadway, including a puddle, which might be hiding a tire-busting pothole.

O If you see debris or a pothole in your lane, don't swerve into the next lane. If you can safely change lanes, do that. If not, you may be able to use the shoulder to get around it. Otherwise, if it's a low item, try to center it between your wheels, as long as you're not getting in the way of other drivers.

O If you *can't* avoid driving over the debris or pothole, grip the wheel firmly and slow down as much as safely possible so you won't lose control of the car.

O When you're safely past the danger, ask a passenger to call local authorities and report the debris or pothole. Or you can do that when you pull over somewhere safe in the future. (Don't use the phone while driving, even for this.)

O If you think your car may be damaged from the impact, pull over as soon as it is safe, and follow the instructions in Chapter 21.

► CHAPTER 20:
Sharing the Road with Everything but Cars

On the road, as in the sports arena, there's always someone bigger than you . . . and someone who's smaller. On the road, you need to be equally concerned about *both* of them. Bigger vehicles can block your view, and they take realllly long to stop. Smaller vehicles can wind up in your blind spot, or they just may not be on your mental radar. Then there are vehicles that are slow, or are oversized, or are constantly starting and stopping (like mail trucks).

While this chapter can't predict *all* the types of vehicles that will cross your path, the tips here will give you some ideas of what to watch for and how to act (and react). Use them—along with your best judgment—to make the best moves.

BE PREPARED TO STOP FOR PEDESTRIANS

If you see people walking near the road you're on, keep an eye on them in case they decide to cross. Don't be surprised when pedestrians ignore the signs and markings meant to help them cross safely. Here are some other guidelines to keep in mind:

- At a stop or yield sign, the pedestrian has the right of way *unless* a police officer tells the driver to go first.

- At a traffic light, if you're waiting to turn right on red, don't go until any pedestrians have finished crossing.

- If a pedestrian is on your side of the road, you may need to come to a stop or slow waaaay down and wait until it's safe to pass them. Always leave tons of room between your car and the pedestrian. In many states, it's OK to cross the double yellow line IF nothing is coming.

- If there's a blind person with a white cane walking on or near the road, know that they have the right of way *every time*.

- Try not to be impatient or rush pedestrians in a crosswalk. You never know their reasons for going slowly. They may have an injury or impairment you can't see.

MAKE SURE MOTORCYCLES ARE ON YOUR RADAR

The size of motorcycles doesn't just make them harder to spot, it also makes it harder to judge how fast they're going or how far away they are.

- Before making any left turn, *actively* look for motorcycles. *Many* motorcycle crashes involve this type of turn!

- Stay an *extra* 1 to 2 seconds behind a motorcycle. On a highway, leave at least 6 seconds and on a slower road, leave about 4 seconds. Stay back even *more* if driving conditions aren't great.

- Don't trust the motorcycle's blinker. Turn signals go off automatically on cars, but not on motorcycles. Always use *your* turn signals so motorcycle riders will know what you're planning (even if you don't see them approaching from behind).

- Expect motorcycles to move around within their lane. Since they can't just drive over a pothole, for example, they might quickly swerve around it.

- Try not to ride *behind* a motorcycle for very long. As a new driver, you'll be less stressed if you don't put yourself in that position.

Myths & Truths

MYTH: Motorcycle crashes happen because of their size and lack of visibility.

TRUTH: The issue may be deeper than that. Some researchers believe that part of the problem is that certain things are just not "on your radar." Because the brain constantly has to filter a ton of input from your five senses, it has to pick and choose what to "notice." On the road, you'll naturally notice cars (because they're the majority of what you see there) and bigger vehicles (because of self-preservation). But that leaves smaller and less-common vehicles like motorcycles in trouble. If we don't actively force ourselves to look for these smaller vehicles (pedestrians, too), we can wind up hurting someone even if we actually looked all around us and *thought* that the coast was clear. In one experiment, researchers found that drivers were twice as likely to notice a taxi as they were to see a motorcycle, even if it was in the exact same spot.

STAY OUT OF THE BLIND SPOTS OF BIG RIGS

Actually, you don't want to hang out too close to *any* big vehicles. The larger the vehicle, the tougher it will be for the driver to see what's around it. Plus, *you* will have trouble seeing around *them*, which can cause you to miss road signs, possible problems, or your next turn. In general, remember that big rigs are tougher to start, stop, and maneuver, so the more you can do to stay out of their way, the better. That said, here are some ways to see and be seen by truckers:

- If you're *behind* a truck, make sure you can see the driver's mirrors. If you can see the driver's face, they can see you.

- If you're behind a truck on an *uphill* road, know that they may slow waaaay down because of the weight. (On downhills, they may pick up speed quicker, too.)

- If you're behind a truck that's *stopped* on a hill in front of you, leave plenty of room in case the truck rolls back when they start up again.

- If you want to *pass* a truck, do it on a straight road and on their left side (where the blind spot is smaller)—and make it quick. Hold the wheel firmly as you drive past in case there's turbulence.

- If you're planning to move in *front* of a truck, don't do it until you are far enough ahead of them that you can see their headlights in your rearview mirror.

- If a truck is trying to pass *you*, don't speed up. Shift as far over in your lane as you can safely, to give them some extra room.

- Watch closely for turn signals on trucks, and make sure you're not on either side of them when they're about to turn.

- If a truck starts moving into your lane where you're driving, don't panic: Judge whether you're better off speeding up (to get past them) or slowing down (to let them in front of you). Use the road's shoulder as an escape route if necessary.

- Oversize loads, buses, and RVs all have the same issues as tractor trailers. With oversize loads, don't try to pass if the "load" is extending outside the lines of their own lane.

------------------ ------------------

Stats & Facts

STAT: Tractor trailers with a full load can weigh 80,000 pounds!

FACT: *Aaaand* . . . it takes them the length of a football field to stop, so don't cut in front of them or hang out too close to their front bumper. If traffic forces you to slow or stop unexpectedly, you want them to have enough time to stop. If not, make sure you have enough room ahead of you as an "escape route" so you can get out of their way.

CLEAR THE ROAD FOR FIRST RESPONDERS

When you see red (or blue and red) lights flashing and hear sirens sounding, you need to get out of the way ASAP. Someone's life may be on the line. Even if the vehicle is coming from the opposite direction, you must do the following (unless they're on the other side of a highway and there's a barrier between them and you).

- Put on your right turn signal, slow down, pull over to the right, and stop. (On a multi-lane one-way road, pull to whatever shoulder or curb is closest to your car.)

- If you *can't* get over or are already stopped, try to get onto a side road up ahead so you can get out of the way.

- If you're approaching an intersection, don't enter it. The emergency vehicle may need to make a turn there, so you should help keep it clear in all directions.

- Emergency vehicles often travel in groups. Once they're all past you, pull back onto the road when it's safe. Wait a bit though. You should leave 500 feet (about 33 car lengths!) between you and them.

- If you see a *stopped* emergency vehicle on or beside the road, reduce your speed and, if possible, move over into a lane that's not next to the vehicle. In many states, this is the law. If there's no way you can safely change lanes, just slow way down.

DON'T HONK AT HORSES (OR FARMERS)

In rural areas, you might find yourself behind a horse and buggy or a piece of farm equipment. Don't honk to get their attention, like you might do with cars and SUVs. It's viewed as rude, and it can scare the animals. Here's what to do instead:

- When you see a slow-moving vehicle ahead, slow down *right away*. Most farm equipment has a max speed of 25 miles per hour, and a horse and buggy goes much, *much* slower. Either way, it only takes seconds for you to wind up *right* behind them.

- Because country roads can be windy, narrow, and bordered by ditches, it may take a while before you can safely pass. Often, the drivers of slow vehicles will move to the side as soon as they can do it safely. So just chill out until they do.

- If there aren't lights on the vehicle, keep an eye on the driver so you can see if they use hand signals. This may be the only way they can let you know they're about to stop or turn.

- If you're stopping *behind* a horse and buggy (like at a traffic light), stay far enough back so you can see the bottom of its rear wheels. Sometimes horses get startled and back up a little when "stopped."

CHECK IT OUT: WHAT'S A "SAFE" FOLLOWING DISTANCE?

Here are some general guides on how much room to leave between you and the vehicle ahead when traveling at a speed of 55 miles per hour. Keep in mind that these guides are for when roads and weather are awesome. Leave more space when things are less perfect.

- ○ **Behind a farm tractor or horse and buggy:** 4 car lengths
- ○ **Behind a snowplow:** 5 car lengths
- ○ **Behind a car:** 16 car lengths (3 1/2 big rigs, or use the 4-second rule)
- ○ **Behind a big rig:** 20 car lengths (4 big rigs)
- ○ **Behind an emergency vehicle:** 33 car lengths (7 big rigs)

➤ CHAPTER 21:
When Your Car Breaks Down

On a good day, your car will start up and keep running until it gets you to your destination. Sadly, there will be times it doesn't work out that way. This chapter covers what to do if you run out of gas, your battery dies, you get a flat tire, or your engine overheats. It also explains how to stay safe while waiting for help or fixing the problem yourself.

FIRST, SOME SAFETY NOTES . . .

Please note that every time we say "pull over," we mean you should put on your flashers and pull over when it's safe to do so, and you should get off the roadway as far as possible. We also mean you should keep your seat belt fastened and doors locked as you phone for help. But if we repeated all these things in every section below, this would be a very long chapter!

Here are a few ways you can get help after getting out of the way of traffic:

- Call your family's roadside assistance service if you have one. If not, you can find help by downloading a free app that will connect you with a nearby towing company.

- Call your family mechanic, if they're fairly close by. Even if they can't help, they may have a suggestion for what to do.

- Call a friend or family member. If you ran out of gas, ask them to bring a full or empty gas can. If they don't have one, just ask for a ride to the gas station, which will probably have a can for sale.

- Call a ride-sharing service to drive you home, so someone there can help you figure out your next move.

- Play it safe if a passerby stops to help. Experts note that it can be dangerous to open your car door (or window) for a stranger, especially if you're in a deserted area. If you need them to phone roadside assistance, you can do this without getting out of your locked car and rolling down the window a crack.

IF YOU RUN OUT OF GAS . . .

EARLY WARNING SIGN: Your "low fuel" light comes on.

IF YOU'RE RUNNING LOW: Pull over and use your phone to search for the nearest gas station using a map app or web browser. Don't just keep going, because the closest fuel may be right behind you, and the "next" one may be miles ahead.

While driving to the station, keep your foot off the gas pedal as much as possible, using it only to maintain a safe speed.

IF YOU RUN OUT: Get off the road ASAP. Don't try to "coast" a little farther, which raises your risk of being rear-ended. Pull off the road as far as possible, and phone for someone to bring you some gas.

NOTE: Even after you put some gas in the tank, it may take a few tries before the car starts. If it still won't turn over, the fuel pump may be damaged, in which case you might need a tow. (Sorry.)

PREVENT IT: Keep at least a quarter tank of gas in your car at all times. Make it more if you're planning a trip that's more than an hour long. If your car's gas gauge is broken, get it fixed ASAP so you'll know when to fill up.

Myths & Truths

MYTH: When the battery light comes on, your battery is dying.

TRUTH: Actually, this can also be a sign that there's a problem with the alternator. You won't be able to drive for very long if the alternator is broken, so seek help from a certified mechanic ASAP. Most mechanics can also put in a new battery, if it turns out that is really all you need.

IF YOUR BATTERY DIES . . .

EARLY WARNING SIGNS: Your engine takes a little extra time to start, it only cranks or clicks when you turn the key, or the headlights are not as bright as usual.

IF YOU'RE RUNNING LOW: Check the age of your battery. There should be a sticker on it with the date it was installed. If it's more than 4 years old, it's probably nearing the end of its life. When you get a new battery, hang onto the warranty in case yours dies before its time.

IF YOUR CAR WON'T START: When you turn the key, if you just hear clicking or if it "cranks" but won't start, you're stuck. Sometimes the dashboard will still light up, which means there's a little juice left.

Your first step should be to try a jump-start. If you have jumper cables and know how to use them, you can do this yourself. If not, call roadside assistance. They'll come even if your car is still in your driveway or a garage!

Once the car is running, have a mechanic check your battery's level and tell you how soon you'll need to replace it. If it's not too bad, they may just tell you to keep the engine running for a certain amount of time (to recharge the battery a bit). You can do that by driving around or by leaving it to idle (in Park) in an open-air location.

PREVENT IT: Whenever you stop the car, make sure you turn off the head-lights, interior lights, radio, and other things that drain the battery, especially if you're not getting out of the car right away. Many people have had a battery die while they sat in a car waiting for a friend!

Replace the battery when recommended by your mechanic. Don't try to get a few more months out of a low battery, especially if there are extreme temperatures outside, which can shorten battery life.

IF YOU HAVE A FLAT TIRE . . .

EARLY WARNING SIGN: Your "low tire pressure" light comes on, or you start to hear thumping noises while driving.

IF YOUR AIR PRESSURE IS LOW: Use a tire gauge or air pump to check the pressure and fill the tires as needed. (Your car's recommended pressure is on a sticker inside the driver's side front door frame.) The tires may just be low because of a change in the weather.

If there's a leak in the tire, it will get low again pretty soon. If that happens—or if you actually see something stuck in the tire— don't drive on it for very long. This puts you at risk for a blowout. Also, driving on a really low tire can damage the metal parts of

the car. Good news: If it's just a nail in your tire, a mechanic may be able to patch the tire, which is way cheaper than buying a new one.

IF YOU HAVE A BLOWOUT: If you hear thumping coming from your tires while driving, pull over ASAP. If a tire blows, the car will suddenly pull to one side, or you'll feel one side of the car suddenly drop. To keep control, DON'T brake, or you could cause a skid. Instead, hold the steering wheel firmly, slowly remove your foot from the gas, and steer slowly to the side of the road. (Also put on your flashers.)

PREVENT IT: Replace your tires before they're too worn down. You can check your tread with the "penny test." Put a penny in the lines of the tire tread, with the top of Lincoln's head poking into the rubber. If the top of his head isn't covered by the tread, you need new tires. (Try this in a few spots on each tire.)

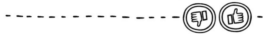

Myths & Truths

MYTH: Add water to the coolant tank to "cure" an overheated engine.

TRUTH: You shouldn't open the coolant tank—or the car's hood—when the engine is hot. You could get burned. Also, water lacks the chemicals that keep things from freezing in winter. If it's cold out, adding water could do more harm than good.

IF YOUR ENGINE OVERHEATS . . .

EARLY WARNING SIGN: The needle on the temperature gauge on your dashboard is closer to the H than the C. The "Check Engine" light may come on, too. If you see steam, it's already overheated.

IF YOUR ENGINE TEMP IS HIGH: Don't wait to see steam. The sooner you act, the less likely you are to have a huge repair bill!

Right away, turn OFF the AC and turn ON the heat. Also put on your flashers and roll down your windows. (AC makes engines hotter, but the heating system pulls heat *away* from the engine.) Pull over and turn off the engine, then call for help.

Do NOT open the hood and/or the cap on the coolant system, and never add coolant to a hot engine. You could wind up getting a nasty burn or cause more damage to the engine.

NOTE: You might be able to add coolant yourself, but you should know that it can take 20 to 60 minutes for the engine to cool down. It may still be better to call for help because there are many reasons for an engine to overheat—and you might need a tow anyway.

PREVENT IT: During routine maintenance like oil changes, ask your mechanic to check the levels of all the fluids, including the coolant/antifreeze. Also check your coolant/antifreeze levels on your own every few weeks. It's super easy: Check your owner's manual for details.

Q&A: Ask Someone Else

- ☐ Who should I call *first* if I have a breakdown? Second? Third?
- ☐ Does my car insurance include a roadside assistance plan? (If not, research and download an app that will help you find roadside assistance nearby.)
- ☐ Can you help me practice changing a tire?
- ☐ Should I accept help from a stranger on the side of the road?

CHECK IT OUT: HOW TO CHANGE A FLAT TIRE

First things first: If you get a flat tire, the safest thing you can do is get off the road ASAP, ideally pulling into a parking lot that's far away from traffic but has plenty of people around. Turn off the car, put it in Park, and set the parking brake. If you're near flowing traffic, also put on your hazard lights.

If you have roadside assistance, of course you'd want to call them: That's why you pay those membership dues! But if you are in a position where you have to do it yourself, follow these basic steps:

GET SET UP

O Get out all of your tire-changing gear. If necessary, use the owner's manual to help you locate and remove the spare tire.

O Secure one of the "good" tires by putting bricks, wedges, or wheel chocks at the front and rear of it, so it can't roll.

REMOVE THE FLAT TIRE

O Pry off the hubcap with a screwdriver or lug wrench.

O Loosen the lug nuts with the wrench, but don't fully remove them.

O Place the car jack under the vehicle frame. (Check the owner's manual for the best spots for this.)

O Jack up the car 6 inches off the ground. (NEVER put any part of your body under the car after it's jacked up!)

O Finish removing the lug nuts. (Place them in a pocket or the hubcap so you don't lose them.)

O Use both hands to pull the tire straight off the bolts.

PUT ON THE SPARE TIRE

O Guide the spare tire onto the bolts.

O Use your fingers to re-thread the lug nuts, then hand-tighten them.

O Use the lug wrench to tighten them more (but not all the way).

O Slowly lower the car, but don't remove the jack yet.

O Follow the directions in the owner's manual on how much more to tighten the lug nuts.

O Put all of your tire-changing gear back in the car, including the flat tire.

O Double-check how fast and how far you can safely drive on the spare. Don't go over that limit, or you might wind up having to change a tire—again!

➤ CHAPTER 22:
Police Warnings, Tickets, and Traffic Court

Even when we're trying our best to follow the rules, we can wind up doing something wrong, such as driving with a broken taillight or going too fast for conditions. So, although we all *hope* we'll never get pulled over by a police officer, it's important to know what to do if it happens.

First of all, stay calm. Breathe. Gradually slow down, put on your turn signal, and pull off the road as far as possible. After coming to a stop, think about what you might have done wrong, just in case they ask, "Do you know why I stopped you?"

Once in a while, you'll get a break: You'll *think* an officer is trying to pull you over, but instead they'll whiz past you on the way to something else. What a feeling!

If that's not the case, though, heed these rules to make the next few minutes as positive as possible:

DON'T MAKE ANY SUDDEN MOVES

Many members of the police force have been hurt and killed at traffic stops, so the officer may be on edge when walking up to your vehicle. To keep everyone calm—and reduce your odds of getting a ticket—do these things after pulling over:

- Turn off the car.
- Turn on an interior light.
- Open your window partway.
- Put your hands on the TOP of the steering wheel.
- Tell the passengers to put their hands on the dashboard or (if they're in the back seat) on the front-seat headrests.
- DON'T get out your driver's license, registration, and proof of insurance until the officer asks for them.

NOTE: You may prefer to keep these items on the passenger seat or console, so you don't have to dig in the glove box. Because glove boxes often contain weapons or tools, keeping yours *closed* can also keep the officer calm.

BE POLITE AND RESPECTFUL

Police officers are 100% allowed to decide whether to give you a ticket or just a warning. The warning could be written or verbal. Basically, they just tell you what you did and that you shouldn't do it again. Being respectful won't guarantee you'll avoid a ticket, but it can't hurt. Some tips are:

Don't get angry (even if you're mad at yourself). Don't argue or make excuses. Don't roll your eyes or make faces. (Keep in mind these may happen automatically, so make it a point to *check* yourself.)

Remind yourself that the officer's goal is to keep the roads safe. As a new driver, you need all the help you can get in that area!

Use your best manners, but don't say much. It's better to give polite one-word responses than to say something that makes things worse.

THE VEHICLE PULLING ME OVER IS UNMARKED. NOW WHAT?

It's less likely to be pulled over by an unmarked police car, but if you're on a dark road and it feels unsafe to pull over or you want to be certain it's a police vehicle flashing you down, you have options. Reduce your speed, turn on your hazards, and then pull over at the nearest well-lit, populated area like a gas station, hospital, or police station. As an added measure, you can call 911 to confirm that the car in question is indeed a police officer.

Myths & Truths

MYTH: An unpaid traffic ticket will wreck your credit score.

TRUTH: Money for traffic tickets is not collected by credit-reporting agencies, so unpaid ones won't affect your credit score. But you are legally obligated to pay parking tickets, and a stash of unpaid parking tickets can affect your license renewal or whether you can register a vehicle.

If you can't afford to pay, look on the ticket for a phone number to call. Ask to talk to someone about a payment plan. This will give you more time to come up with the cash.

DON'T KEEP IT A SECRET

When you get a warning or ticket, you will *wish* you didn't have to tell your parents or whoever is responsible for you, but it's important that you do. You'll show that you're being honest, which goes a long way toward building trust. Responsible adults can also help you decide what to do next—to pay or to go to court—and can help you get a lawyer, if needed.

Finally, explain what happened and ask what you could do better next time. (Or tell them what you'll do differently, if you already know.)

They'll probably find out anyway, and it's better for them to hear it from you first.

IF YOU WIND UP WITH A TICKET . . .

First, know that *signing* the ticket is not the same as saying you're guilty. It's just saying you agree to either pay the fine or go to court. (Though you should read the whole thing.) Kind of like signing when you get a package—you're saying, "Yes, I got it."

Usually, the ticket will say what your offenses were, what your fines are, and what choices you have for dealing with it.

Most states also have a points system, where you earn points every time you do something wrong. If you get a certain number of points, you'll lose your license for a while. Sometimes these points can raise your car insurance rates. People who go to court will usually wind up with a lower penalty, so talk to your parents before you pay up. Going to traffic school can sometimes remove points from your license, too.

CHECK IT OUT: KNOW YOUR RIGHTS

Let's say you think you might have done something seriously wrong. Like worse than speeding. Or maybe you just *look* like you did because your passengers are knuckleheads or someone left illegal stuff in your car. Either way, if you think you might be headed toward an *arrest*, keep these things in mind. (Luckily, the guidelines are a lot like what you've seen a bazillion times on TV.)

○ Don't say or sign anything.

○ Let the officer know you want to invoke your right to remain silent. Your passengers can invoke that right, too. They can *also* ask for permission to leave.

○ Officers can only search your car if they *see* something sketchy.

○ Officers cannot search your cell phone without your permission. (Obviously, a lawyer would advise against that.)

○ If you are being held or arrested, you have the right to make one phone call.

If you call a *lawyer*, the police aren't allowed to listen in. If you call your *parents*, they can eavesdrop. Even if you didn't do anything wrong, anything you say can and will be held against you. Yeah, just like on TV. So don't say any more than you have to.

➤ CHAPTER 23:

Accidents Happen . . .
So You Should Know
What to Do

It's scary to be in an accident. As with anything, knowing what to do *next* can make it easier for you to get the help you need while staying safe and calm (or as calm as possible).

MAKE SURE YOU'RE AS SAFE AS POSSIBLE

Turn on your flashers ASAP and, if your car is drivable, pull off the road as far as you can. (You may want to take some photos first if it doesn't put you at risk.)

If your car *isn't* drivable, get yourself and your passengers to safety—far, far away from the car accident. You don't want to get hurt if a distracted driver swerves in your direction or strikes your poor car.

If someone is injured, though, do NOT move them unless there's a danger of the vehicle catching on fire. Moving an injured person can cause added harm.

CALL 911 (OR ASK SOMEONE ELSE TO)

Even if the accident seems very minor, you should call the police. In some states, it's the law. Even if that's not the case where you live, having the police there can help protect you from road-rage drivers. Also, you've probably never had to deal with any accident-related things before! Police officers do it all the time. They can help guide you through the next steps.

BREATHE AND DO A WELLNESS CHECK

While you wait for help, think about how you're feeling. Mentally scan your body from head to toe. Keep in mind you may be a little in shock. So also look yourself over for signs of injuries. You don't want to do a lot of moving around if you *have* gotten hurt. Ask any passengers how they're doing, too. Help should arrive quickly, and EMTs can get to work more quickly if you can tell them who's hurt and where.

TRADE INFO WITH THE OTHER DRIVER

If everyone is OK, your next step is to get out of the car and exchange insurance info with the other driver. (See "Check It Out" at the end of this chapter.)

DON'T talk about who was at fault or what happened. That includes blaming yourself OR the other driver! That could come back to bite you later.

Don't do anything that puts you or others at risk, though. For example, if the other driver is very angry or agitated—stay buckled in and try not to say or do anything to get them more upset. If you're on a busy highway, you may be safer staying buckled up until the police arrive.

STAY CALM AROUND FIRST RESPONDERS

Once help arrives, it can stir up emotions again. The first responders will probably ask you lots of questions to see if you need to go to a hospital to get checked out. The police will ask a lot of questions, too. This is not the time to argue or to be angry. The calmer you can be, the better things are likely to go for you.

Also know that sometimes a police officer will give one of the drivers a citation (ticket). If they do not, it may be because they're not sure who caused the crash.

Myths & Truths

MYTH: You have to give a statement to the other driver's insurance company.

TRUTH: Actually, you don't. You do have to talk to *your* insurer, but legally you don't have to talk to *theirs*. Sometimes it's a good idea to share your side of the story—like if you think the other driver may be bending the truth. But first talk to your insurance agent, your parents, and your lawyer (if you have one) about what and how much to say. The less you talk, the less your words can get twisted.

Also, know you don't have to talk to the other *driver* after the accident. They might call you (since you traded phone numbers). If so, just tell them to call your insurance agent instead. That's what you're paying the insurance company for. Plus, it keeps personal feelings out of the equation.

LET YOUR PARENTS KNOW WHAT'S UP

It's the same story as with traffic tickets: You don't want your parents to find out about your accident from anyone but *you*. Plus, they've likely been in some fender benders, too, so hopefully they won't get too upset.

If someone is waiting for you at your destination, you may want to give them a call, too, so they'll know you're not going to make it. If you don't have time for that, ask your parents or a passenger to take care of the call.

GET ON THE PHONE WITH YOUR INSURER

Many people don't call their insurer until they get home. Since you're a new driver, and this is likely your first accident, you may want to call while you're at the scene. Unlike everyone else at the site of the crash, the insurer's people are "on your side," and they'll help you make sure you say and do what you should. This can save you some headaches later. Their number will be on your insurance card, but it's a good idea to put it in your phone contacts *before* you get in an accident.

- - - - - - - - - - - - - - - ☑ - - - - - - - - - - - - - - -

Stats & Facts

STAT: Your accident report should be available in 3 to 7 days.

FACT: Get a copy of the accident report ASAP and read it over thoroughly to make sure there aren't any mistakes. Sometimes police officers switch up the drivers' names or whose car is whose. They may not have passenger names listed. Their diagrams or drawings may be mislabeled. They weren't actually there when the accident happened, after all.

If you see any errors, call the officer right away, while the whole thing is fresh in your mind. (The officer's name and contact info will be on the report, too.) Don't expect the officer to make any changes, even if it's wrong. But if they do, ask for a copy of the "revised" report, and double-check it, too.

- -

KNOW WHAT TO EXPECT NEXT

This is the best part: Your insurance company will deal with the *other* driver from now on, so you don't have to. That said, you might need to have a few conversations with your insurance agent before this is all done.

First, the agent will want all of the notes and photos you collected at the scene, as well as your version of what happened.

You should ask the agent some questions, too. Find out what your insurance will cover and ask what you'll need to pay. Many insurance companies will pay for a rental car, but usually people under 21 years old aren't allowed to drive rentals. Still, your *parents* may want to take advantage of the rental if it's offered.

If you have any medical bills—for example, if you got an X-ray of your wrist or something—you need to give the bills to the insurance company, too. They will be part of the claim, so they shouldn't be paid by your health insurance company.

Again, this is why it's a good idea to put aside your ego and ask your parents to help guide you. Don't back out of the process, though, even if they're OK with taking over. By staying involved, you'll get a better idea of what to do if something like this happens again.

WHAT TO DO AFTER A HIT-AND-RUN

Whenever there is an accident, both drivers need to stay at the scene and go through all of the above steps, even if it's a minor incident (like a parking lot fender bender). Failing to report an accident can get you in trouble if the other driver reports it later on. (That may make it look like your fault, even if it's not.) Leaving the scene before police arrive is even *worse*, especially if someone was hurt. Penalties can include fines, a suspended license, and even jail time. Even if you're freaked out and wish you could run away, it's really important for you to stay put.

What if you're the victim of a hit-and-run? Don't try to chase down the other driver. You risk facing road rage or getting in another accident because you're so upset. Don't give up and leave, either. You'll want to file a report with the police. If you don't, the other driver can get home, call their insurance agent, and tell them a story that makes *you* look like the bad guy!

After you call 911, write down as many details as you can, while they're fresh in your mind. The most helpful ones would be the license plate number, make, model, and color of the other vehicle, as well as what damage you think their car may have had (like a broken headlight or side mirror). Also note the exact date, time, and location of the accident, as well as the direction that the other driver was traveling when they left. Finally, take notes on what happened during the accident itself. If there are any witnesses, see if they remember something you missed, and ask them to stay until the police arrive. Keep in mind that many outdoor public areas have cameras, which can help police track down the other driver.

CHECK IT OUT: INFO TO COLLECT AT AN ACCIDENT SCENE

Before you start gathering info, keep in mind that your first goal is to be *safe*. If you aren't sure you can do any of the following without putting yourself in harm's way, just wait until police arrive. They will help redirect traffic and get you all to a safe spot to talk.

Also, don't talk too much! You don't want anyone to be able to make it look like you're at fault if you're not. Even if you think you are, you might be wrong. So save the apologies and stick to this list:

USE YOUR CAMERA TO TAKE A PHOTO OR VIDEO OF:

- O The accident scene (from many angles), including landmarks and street signs
- O The damage to your car and to the other driver's car
- O The other driver's license plate number
- O The make, model, and color of their vehicle
- O Their driver's license and insurance card
- O Eyewitness videos stating what they saw

TRADE THIS INFO WITH THE OTHER DRIVER:

- O Full name
- O Phone number
- O Address
- O Driver's license number
- O License plate number
- O Insurance company and policy number

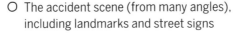

ASK PASSENGERS AND EYEWITNESSES FOR:

O Full name

O Phone number

O Address

O A description of what they saw (Take notes or video them!)

ASK THE POLICE OFFICERS FOR:

O Full name

O Badge number

O Car number

NOTE: As soon as possible, go over all your notes. Write down everything you can remember or record yourself saying it on video. You might *think* you'll never forget a minute of this stressful situation, but you'd be surprised at how fast the details fade. And the more details you can give your insurance agent (and lawyer, if necessary), the better they can help you.

CHECK IT OUT: WHAT TO DO IF YOU WITNESS AN ACCIDENT

The more you're out there driving, the more likely
it is that you'll someday see an accident happen.
Here's some guidance on what to do (or not):

○ Make sure you're safe—don't do anything to put yourself at risk. That includes calling 911 if you're driving. If there are lots of other people around, let them call 911. If not, find a safe place to pull off the road before you dial. Make sure you're away from the crash by at least 100 feet. (That's more than the length of a big rig.) Also NEVER get out to check on the victims if it puts you at risk.

○ If you do call 911, say "I saw a car accident." Then tell them where it is and answer any other questions they have.

○ Wait for the police to arrive and answer any questions they have. Only give facts, not guesses or opinions. Know that you may be called up later to share your story again, so it's a good idea to write down what you remember ASAP.

▶ CHAPTER 24:
How to Make Sure You're Safe to Drive

Is your car in good working order? Check. Is the gas tank full? Check. Are the windows and mirrors clean? Check. As you go through your mental checklist of what needs to be "good to go" before you hit the road, don't forget to check *yourself*.

Is your *body* in good working order? Did you fuel up with enough sleep? Is your brain clear so you can focus?

Taking the wheel if you're not in top form can put you (and others) at serious risk. So can riding with someone who is not as focused as they should be.

While you're probably thinking we're going to talk about alcohol and drugs, they're not first on the list here. They are serious issues, but you already know that. Instead, we are starting with some of the more *surprising* things that affect your ability to drive safely. Check them out . . .

SCHEDULE YOUR OWN ROUTINE MAINTENANCE

Doing routine maintenance on your car means your mechanic can find and fix problems sooner—hopefully so you won't break down on a deserted highway. Your body also needs regular checkups to look for possible issues, including ones that can affect your ability to drive safely.

For starters, you should get regular vision and hearing tests—once a year or whenever your doctor recommends it. Vision can change a lot in just a few months, or it may happen so slowly you don't notice. The same can be true with hearing. You can ask your pediatrician or doctor to check your hearing when you get your flu shot. You can also go see an audiologist (hearing doctor) if people keep telling you they have to repeat themselves. (Only you know if you are just *ignoring* them!)

Finally, if you get hurt—in sports or gym class, for example—ask your doctor if there will be any limits on your driving. That may happen because of physical restrictions (like crutches or a cast) or because of medicines (we'll get to that in a second).

Even something like a twisted ankle or sore knee can make it tough to maneuver from the gas to the brake. So even if your injury doesn't send you to the doctor, at least be honest with yourself about whether you can drive safely.

DOUBLE-CHECK THE SIDE EFFECTS OF MEDICINES

Most people don't really think of drugstore medicines as "drugs." After all, you can buy them right off the shelf without a prescription. But even common medicines can affect people's ability to drive, just like illegal drugs and alcohol do.

Some of the biggest offenders are cold, flu, and allergy medicines, including antihistamines, decongestants, and cough medicines, as well as sleep aids. But other medications, including prescription meds like those taken for depression and anxiety, can make you a little woozy when you first begin taking them.

Whenever you start taking *any* kind of medicine, read the labels for warnings, or ask your doctor or pharmacist if you can safely drive while taking it. Don't rely on your parents for this information: You'll have to figure it out for yourself someday, so it might as well be now.

TIP: If the label says not to operate "heavy machinery" while taking something, that means your car—not just a forklift or backhoe.

DON'T DRIVE WHEN YOU'RE DROWSY

Teens and college students are notorious for getting too little sleep. It's no secret why: School starts too early, activities run too late, and then there's all the *homework.*

Problem is, drowsy driving means you have a slower reaction time, you can't see as clearly, and you have more trouble concentrating. In fact, if you're only getting 6 hours of sleep at night, you're operating as if you have a blood alcohol level of 0.1 percent!

You might be shocked to know that sleep experts recommend that you should be getting at least 8 hours of sleep at ages 16 and 17 and at least 7 hours if you're 18 or older.

That may seem unrealistic, but you should try to think of where you can readjust your schedule to gain a little more sleep time. Maybe you can be less of a perfectionist with your homework. Or maybe you can get off the video game server sooner. You're not going to excel at memorizing equations or sinking pirate ships if you're exhausted anyway. Or maybe you can nap in study hall? Get creative so you can get as much sleep as possible.

See "Check It Out" for a list of symptoms that can lead to drowsy driving.

LEARN THE TRUTH ABOUT SOBERING UP

How many drinks are OK if you're the driver? Short answer: None. Even if a driver's blood alcohol level is just *half* the legal limit, their crash risk is up to 7 times higher.

(Obviously, for people under 21, the answer is none *anyway.* But we're not going to pretend that everyone follows the rules.)

Alcohol reduces concentration, affects judgment, and slows reaction time—all of which are *already* an issue for new drivers. It also boosts risk-taking *and* confidence, which is not a great combo. Basically, you'll think you're doing some awesome driving, even when you're absolutely *not.*

If you're riding with a legal adult, keep an eye on their drinking, too. They should not have more than 1 drink per hour. That's how long it takes for the body to process alcohol. And people with lower bodyweight usually need a little longer to sober up.

Finally, don't buy the myths that drinking coffee or taking a shower will speed up the sobering process. The only thing that helps alcohol wear off is *time*.

DON'T BELIEVE THE MYTHS ABOUT DRUGS

It's a common myth that people who smoke marijuana are OK to drive. In reality, though, pot can slow reaction time, affect coordination, and make it tougher to judge time and distance. That makes it riskier when trying to pull into traffic, among other things. Smoking pot while driving is even worse: Like cigarette smoking and vaping, it takes one of your hands off the wheel, and if you drop a lit butt in your lap, you could end up doing all kinds of weird swerving.

"Stimulant" drugs are no better. Cocaine and meth, for example, are linked to aggressive and reckless driving. We don't have to tell you that's not good.

Mixing drugs and alcohol is even *worse*. So is drinking alcohol and taking certain prescription or drugstore medicines. Obviously, any combo of "bad" ideas is going to be a "worse" idea. It's basic math.

KNOW THE RISKS OF "IMPAIRED" DRIVING

As if your safety and the safety of your passengers weren't enough, driving while "impaired" can do a lot to wreck your driving record and future prospects for work. For example, even if you *don't* wind up causing an accident, just getting stopped while under the influence of anything (or driving drowsy) can result in fines, the loss of your license, higher insurance rates, job loss, jail time, and a criminal record.

You've probably heard it a million times already: Your generation is very lucky—you can call a ride-sharing service almost anywhere in the country! If not, you can call your parents for a ride. You might *think* they'd be cranky about having to come get you, but most parents will actually be relieved you used good judgment when it really mattered.

CHECK IT OUT: WHAT'S YOUR SCORE FOR DROWSY DRIVING?

Many people can't tell if they're about to nod off at the wheel—
but 37 percent of Americans do it every year. (Yikes!)

Below are some of the signs that you're too tired to drive.
Don't get behind the wheel if you're experiencing these
symptoms—and if they start to happen while you're driving, pull over ASAP and take a nap or call an Uber.

- O Yawning
- O Eye-rubbing
- O Squinting to try to "focus"
- O Blinking fast and often
- O "Heavy" eyelids
- O Wandering thoughts
- O Spacing out
- O Head bobbing
- O Drifting sideways in your lane
- O Feeling cranky and restless

➤ CHAPTER 25:
Car Maintenance for Non-Mechanics

Not exactly interested in how cars *work*? That's OK. Not everyone is. But you at least need to know what types of service need to happen (and when).

Waiting too long to do maintenance or repairs can result in bigger (and costlier) problems. For example, if you let your oil filter get too dirty, the oil won't be able to keep the engine running smoothly. Or driving on overly worn tires can make you more likely to skid off the road in bad weather. You get the picture.

Check your owner's manual for the specific timing of things like oil changes, tire rotation, etc. But first, check out the things listed here, which are easy to do, even if you're not mechanically minded.

SWITCH OUT OLD WIPER BLADES

It's easy to tell when your windshield wiper blades are ready for the trash: When it rains, they leave streaks. You can also test them in nice weather by spritzing on some wiper fluid and watching them work.

Your owner's manual should tell you what kind of blades you need. Or you can go to an auto parts store and tell them what type of car you have (make, model, and year), and they'll figure it out.

Many shops will even replace them for you for free; they just come out into the parking lot with you after you pay, then swap them out. If not, don't worry. Wiper blades are super easy to remove and replace by yourself.

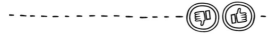

Myths & Truths

MYTH: Oil needs to be changed every 3,000 miles.

TRUTH: That was before synthetic oil. Now you can go anywhere from 5,000 to 10,000 miles before needing an oil change.

Usually, mechanics will put a decal on the windshield that tells you when your next oil change is due. If your car's computer monitors the oil life *for* you, it might display something on the dashboard that indicates when you need an oil change. If you don't drive very much, that may be *months* after the little sticker suggests you make an appointment.

FILL 'ER UP WITH IMPORTANT FLUIDS

Windshield washer fluid and coolant/antifreeze are two fluids that are pretty simple to top off. The plastic containers that hold them are easy to get to once you pop the hood. They're also easy to

open and fill up to the "fill to here" line.

The trickiest part is making sure you prop up the hood properly using the "hood prop rod." You may need to check the owner's manual to figure out where to insert the end, since hoods can have lots of weird markings and holes on their underside.

TEST YOUR TIRE TREADS WITH A PENNY

As mentioned in Chapter 21, you can easily see if you need new tires. Simply insert a penny into the tire tread, with the top of Lincoln's head poking into the rubber. If you can see the *top* of Lincoln's head, the tire's tread is getting dangerously worn. That means you'll have less traction, so you'll be more likely to slide around on the road. Worn tires can also put you at risk for blowouts, which can make you lose control of the car. If you need new tires, don't wait, especially if it's before winter, when roads are more likely to be slippery.

MAKE SURE YOUR LIGHTS ARE LIT

Too often, we don't realize we have a headlight out because we're inside the car when they're on. But burnt-out lights make it tougher for drivers to see you—and you can get pulled over and ticketed over for it. Every month or so, ask a friend to help you check if all of your lights work, including blinkers, headlights, high beams, turn signals, and flashers.

Switching out a burnt bulb is something you can probably do on your own, too, though they're easier to get at in some cars than in others. Make sure you buy the right bulb, though: They're not all the same—even in the same car.

Another way to brighten your view is to get a headlight-cleaning kit to get rid of any haze or yellowness on the plastic coverings. This is more common in older cars, since the damage is caused by UV rays.

Myths & Truths

MYTH: If you don't go to the dealer for maintenance, you'll void your car's warranty.

TRUTH: If you want a *repair* to be *covered* by your warranty, you'll need to have that work done at the dealership. But you can get oil changes and other checkups done wherever you like. Sometimes, dealerships will provide free maintenance for at least the first few visits, because they want you to get in the habit of coming back to them. Check your car's paperwork to see if that's the case.

CHECK WHAT'S UNDER WARRANTY

A warranty is a legal guarantee that the manufacturer will replace or repair certain things—free of charge—if they break within a certain timeframe. Often, new cars will have "bumper to bumper coverage" for 36 months or 36,000 miles (whichever comes first). If you bought a used car, the original warranty will transfer along with it. Sometimes used-car dealers also offer an added warranty of their own to make you feel better about buying a new-to-you ride.

Another wrinkle: Different car parts may have a longer warranty than others. The rust-proof coating may be guaranteed for 10 years, for example. And when you buy a new battery or tires, those will come with their own warranties, too.

To make sure you know what's covered, use a file or envelope to store all the paperwork and receipts for any car parts, maintenance, and repair work. Hold onto these materials until you sell the car. They won't take up much space, and you may get more money for the car if you can show how well you maintained it.

DON'T GET CHEATED BY CHEATY CHEATERS

We love auto mechanics! They are our heroes when they get our "baby" running smoothly after something goes wrong. But you've probably heard plenty of stories about people getting ripped off. So how do you avoid that?

Your parents probably have their own favorite mechanic. But if you ever have to find your own, look for ones who have *certifications*. The National Institute for Automotive Service Excellence (ASE) offers the Certified Master Automotive Technician status, which needs to be renewed every few years. Some automakers and dealerships provide their own training and certifications that are specific to their brands. This can help you find a mechanic who will really understand your type of vehicle.

To make sure you're paying a fair price, just type "car repair estimate" in the search bar of your favorite browser. There are lots of websites where you can plug in repair info and see what most people are paying for it. If you're ever feeling skeptical, know that it's fine to get a second opinion.

SIGN UP FOR MESSAGES ABOUT RECALLS

Recalls happen when the National Highway Traffic Safety Administration decides something about a vehicle is not safe enough. The manufacturer is then required to fix it for the owners for *free* or, in rare cases, buy back the whole car. To get the repairs done, though, you need to *know* there's a recall in the first place.

If you're the first owner of a car, you'll get those notices automatically, but you may not get them if you bought the car used. To make sure you get the news about recalls for your car, visit the NHTSA website (nhtsa.gov) and click on the Recalls tab. There, you'll be able to check for existing problems and sign up for emails about future ones.

MAKE ROUTINE MAINTENANCE A NO-BRAINER

Every vehicle is different, and each one is driven in different places for different lengths of time. Dusty roads, long commutes, riding the brakes . . . all kinds of things can affect how long various car parts will last.

The general recommendations for your vehicle will be spelled out clearly in the owner's manual. But there's an easier approach: Take your car for a *full-service* oil change every 5,000 to 10,000 miles. This means the mechanic will also check and top off fluids and check the lights, suspension, and many other features. (Ask for a list of what's included.) Some states also require an annual inspection for safety and/or emissions. If you live in one of those states, you're guaranteed that your car will get a good once-over each year.

Another way to make it easier on yourself? Find a dealer or mechanic who is certified to work on your type of car and go to them consistently. They will keep track of what is getting done, and they'll alert you when it's time to do something—including extras, like rotating the tires.

With all the things you have to keep in mind as a new driver, it's nice to be able to leave this stuff to the experts.

CHECK IT OUT:
GET MORE MILEAGE OUT OF YOUR AUTO PARTS

Here's a quick reference list of common things that need replacing—and how long they usually last. Check your owner's manual and auto parts packaging, though. Cheaper brands can wear out sooner! It might be worth it to pay more for a specific part if it means replacing it less often.

O 5,000 to 10,000 miles: oil filter

O 10,000 miles: wiper blades

O 15,000 miles: air filter

O 30,000 miles: fuel filter

O 50,000 to 60,000 miles: battery, brake pads, brake rotors, hoses, belts

O 60,000 to 75,000 miles: spark plugs

O 75,000 to 90,000 miles: timing belt

A FINAL NOTE: ENJOY THE JOURNEY

Many of the adults you know have driven hundreds of thousands of miles. They've probably been driving for longer than you've been *alive*. That's why they seem so confident, comfortable, and chill when they're behind the wheel.

You'll get there, too—and sooner than you realize. (Think about all the twentysomethings you know who are totally fine with driving a few hours to their college or to the beach!)

The tips in this book are meant to help you get up to speed quicker, but that doesn't mean you should rush into anything. Driving is an exciting freedom, but it's also an enormous responsibility. So ease into it. Savor this moment. And lean on your parents and driving instructors when you need help.

By going at your own speed, you'll be able to enjoy every mile of your journey.

INDEX

ABOUT THE AUTHOR

Kristy Grant is a writer from Hoboken, New Jersey. In her spare time, she enjoys planting vegetables in her garden and reading stories about the great open road.

PHONE NUMBERS & EMERGENCY CONTACTS

_____

_____

_____

_____

_____

_____

_____

_____

_____

_____

_____

_____

_____

_____

_____